Get the Look

Photography by
Ray Main

Get the Look

How to be a stylist in your own home

Rebecca Tanqueray

Kyle Cathie Limited

First published in Great Britain in 2000 by

Kyle Cathie Limited

122 Arlington Road

London NW1 7HP

ISBN 1 85626 372 X

Text © 2000 Rebecca Tanqueray

Photography © 2000 Ray Main/Mainstream except for those listed on p. 158

Commissioning Editor: Kate Oldfield

Production: Lorraine Baird and Sha Huxtable

Design: Button Design Company

A CIP catalogue record for this title is available from the British Library

Colour separations by Colourscan, Singapore

Printed and bound in Toledo, Spain by Artes Graficas

D.L. TO: 1480-2000

Contents

Introduction   6

What is a stylist? What do they do? How can we learn their tricks
of the trade when arranging our own homes?

1 Keep it Simple   14

How to pare down and purify your living space using storage,
colour, texture or just one big idea. Plus four easy-to-do quick fixes.

2 Display   52

How to show off your possessions for maximum impact and
where to do it. Plus new ideas for displaying flowers and five
quick fixes.

3 Lateral Thinking   106

How to use unconventional ideas, objects and materials to great
effect all around the home. Plus a hit list of the suppliers the
stylists use and eight quick fixes.

4 Fashion Statement   136

How to keep your interior up to date inexpensively by using
catwalk fabrics, trendy trimmings or even by bringing your clothes
out of the closet. Plus six fashionable fixes.

Index   156

Acknowledgements   158

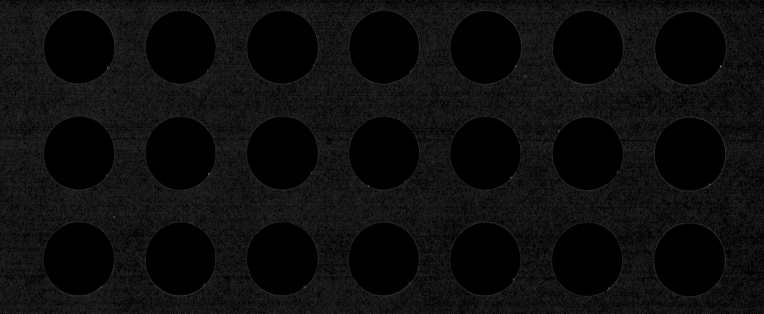

Introduction

'Get the look' is an expression that has become part of the lexicon of the lifestyle media in recent years. As features editors in television and the press hone in on the home, bombarding us with images of beautiful, aspirational interiors, this little phrase is sure to follow one step behind, persuading us that if we follow the prescribed formula, our homes can look just as good.

It's a promise that appeals to most of us. Who wouldn't want a living space filled with just the right amount of just the right things; one of those stylish and sophisticated homes that look, well, so little like our own. And rather than admit defeat, we eagerly devour those get-the-look columns in the vain hope that a simple shopping list will turn our homes into temples of cutting-edge taste.

It doesn't work like this in real life, of course. While a quota of fashionable furniture will impress our impressionable friends, no amount of the stuff can bring us instant style. Stylishness, happily, has a far more democratic, far more elusive quality that has less to do with the contents of our homes (in value terms, that is) than with the way in which we treat them.

While it is reassuring to realize that we don't need limitless funds to make our homes look good, this also poses a new challenge. If we can't buy ourselves cutting-edge credentials, how can we make our homes stylish? What do we need to do to create the kind of interior we crave?

The solution, it seemed to me when I began this book, was to ask the experts – the interior stylists who have made a profession out of making homes

look good for the camera. Their innovative ideas and creative vision lie at the heart of those aspirational magazine interiors, so by tapping into their thought processes, by discovering their tricks of the trade, I felt we would have the key to successful styling.

It would be glib to suggest that there is a formula for this kind of creativity, but there is much we can learn from the stylist's approach that will have an instant impact on our homes. The first is to start thinking visually; to take a fresh look at every aspect of our surroundings, from the furniture and furnishings down to the smallest mantelpiece or tabletop display. Those cutting-edge looks can come from the simplest finishing touches: a row of graphic ceramics, for example, or a single brilliant flower in a plastic bottle.

The second is to have the courage to be creative. What makes a 'styled' interior stand out from the rest is often a strong visual idea, so keep your home in mind wherever you are and be open to inspiration. It can come from anywhere – the colours of a painting, the display in a shop window, a collection of objects found on a beach. A stylist will feed off any kind of visual material and often the more unexpected the stimulus of an interior scheme, the more striking the result.

The professional stylist, of course, has an advantage over the amateur. Working in the field, he or she will be well aware of what the current interior trends are and will easily be able to bring a cutting-edge flavour to a space. The rest of us will need to seek out that information, but these days it is easily done. Browse through interiors books, magazines or internet sites to get a feel of what you like or visit current design exhibitions and trendy furniture shops to discover the latest looks for the home. Be discerning and try to avoid the fads – you shouldn't buy anything just because it is fashionable.

Finally, one word of warning. It's vital to take on board the fact that you are creating an environment for yourself and that only by choosing things you like will you achieve a look that works. Today's trendy interior is a very personal space, so be inspired by the homes you read about but don't be tempted to try to replicate them exactly or you will end up living in an up-to-the-minute interior that has none of you in it. The most striking homes are those with a strong sense of identity and an individual style. This is what the stylist's approach, and this book, should help you to find.

"Keeping the background simple allows me to change my interior whenever I like." Janie Jackson

To many, styling is what you do to a room once it's complete – the icing on the cake, if you like. It's about adding the finishing touches to an interior – the tassel on the curtain, the flowers in the vase, the champagne glass on the table – to make it ready for the camera. But to view styling like this is to misunderstand it, particularly today. While a decade or so ago stylists tended to go overboard, accessorizing interiors with fussy details, these days they are more likely to take things away. Why? Because the good stylist has learnt what the rest of us need to: less stuff simply looks better.

'Keep it simple' is the contemporary stylist's first rule of thumb, whatever the project in hand. Whether the brief is to create a cutting-edge living room for a magazine or to produce a brochure for a department store, what she or he will be after is a clean and graphic image that will grab the eye and the attention. Think of the lifestyle photographs that seduce us today: the sculptural chair against a plain plaster wall; the bedside table without bedside clutter; the solitary ceramic vase on a mantelpiece. These images work because they are simple and uncomplicated.

You might argue, of course, that the current appetite for pared-down living spaces is purely the result of media mindwashing; that it is only because we are bombarded with simple images in the design press that we now crave simplicity in the home. It's true that the simple look has not always been so sought-after, but it is not just the media that has made us minimalists. After decades of materialism, it seems that we are beginning to see the truth in that old maxim 'less is more' and recognizing the need to downshift both our lives and our decoration.

The home has taken on the role of antidote to the stressful, product-swamped world outside, and our requirements of it have changed. We want it to be fashionable, yes, but we also need it to be an emotional and visual refuge, somewhere calm and easy on the eye. And what we have learnt from the stylist's art is that by reducing the elements in a room, by giving objects the space to breathe, by – in essence – keeping things simple, we can create the perfect uncluttered contemporary space and up the visual impact of an interior instantly. Now it's time to do it in our own homes.

Keep It Simple

Wanting to maximise the light which floods her London home, stylist Janie Jackson kept colour and decoration to a minimum. In the sitting room (left) the floors were stripped, walls painted white or soft green and windows simply hung with swathes of diaphanous fabric. Although the furniture too, was reduced to essentials, the room doesn't feel bare or uncomfortable but unfussy and feminine with pretty details, such as a glass chandelier, adding a decorative edge. The simple furnishing scheme and soft pastel palette were also carried through into the bedrooms (top, far left).

A wash of white, the downstairs dining and sitting area of stylist Janie Jackson's home is simple but striking (right and far right, top). By eliminating clutter, by using a monotone colour scheme and by arranging furniture with a symmetrical eye, she has achieved a look which is clean-lined, pared down and very impactful. Even the incense holder – a monolithic block of wood – is simplicity itself (above).

Conceal the Clutter

Paring Down

A reductive approach to furnishing – or the technique of taking things away rather than adding to them – may sound simple in theory but can prove more difficult in practice. It is one thing to admire the bare and beautiful living spaces we see in magazines and on television, but quite another to attempt to create something similar ourselves. For a start, where can we stash all that domestic clutter: the piles of paper, the children's toys? And how can we justify getting rid of furniture we bought just a few years ago? More to the point, how can we fail to be seduced into acquiring more and more possessions when our doormats are deluged with catalogues urging us towards the next best buy? To master the skill of 'paring down', the trick is to adopt an entirely different approach to furnishing your home.

First, opt out of the consumer rat race and put a stop to your shopping. It won't be easy. We have been schooled in a commercial culture and it's hard to shake off the belief that stuffing your home with designer objects and accessories will automatically make it stylish. It won't. While a well-chosen piece of fashionable furniture or fabric will, of course, do any interior a favour, by swamping your home with all the latest must-haves, you will be buying yourself a look that is certain to date and diluting the visual impact of what you buy. Remember, less stuff looks better.

The next hurdle is reducing what you already have in the home. The solution here is to take things gradually and not to feel you have to go too far. Getting rid of the odd unwanted or dated item can be very therapeutic, but don't feel you have to throw away everything. It is just as important to decide what to keep as what to remove. Rather than stripping your home of possessions, the trick is to create somewhere simple but not stark, uncluttered but not uninteresting.

How To Achieve This

Don't live with what you don't love. Dispose of any items that aren't really 'you': the hand-me-down furniture you accepted because it was free; the second-hand curtains you always meant to replace; the wedding-present cruet set you would never have bought yourself. Other people's taste is questionable at the best of times, so why make do with it in your own home? Take a step back, really take stock of what you've got and do away with anything you don't like or don't need.

Dawna Walter, founder of storage emporium The Holding Company, has made a profession out of ordering people's lives and urges her clients to be ruthless: anything that hasn't been worn for two years should be discarded, she declares, and nothing should be hung on to 'just in case'. This kind of possession purge may not come easily to those of us with a make-do-and-mend mentality, but stripping your home of the unwanted and the unloved is crucial if you are to create an uncluttered and personal living space. And there is no reason to feel guilty: what is junk to you may be a gem to someone else and if you donate your cast-offs to charity shops or friends, for example, you will be doing yourself and someone else a favour.

Ideas for Clutter-free Living

Living rooms

- Buy colourful cable turtles to hide trailing wires.
- Invest in an attractive rack for your magazines and recycle any that you've finished reading.
- Keep your mantelpiece under control. Invitations can be pegged together or stuffed into a toast rack for instant sculpture.
- Buy big bookshelves: they will look good even if they are half empty.
- Keep anything unsightly (videos, tapes, remote controls, etc.) out of sight.

Kitchens

- Make the most of high ceilings by setting up hanging racks for pans and utensils.
- Keep the worktop clear. Things you use regularly (oils, coffee, salt, etc.) should be concealed in cupboards or lined up on a shelf.
- Keep your spices out of sight (they last longer in the dark) or in a tidy row of uniform non-transparent storage jars.

Offices

- In- and out-trays are a must. Nothing makes an office look messier than stacks of paper.

Paring Down

Storage is the key to uncluttered contemporary living, so make sure you have enough of it in your home. Don't just stick to built-in cupboards and strip shelving, choose stylish pieces of display furniture, such as this swivelling stack of wooden cubes (left), which look good in themselves and which can also accommodate all manner of bits and pieces. And don't forget the details. Boxes and baskets (above) can do much to help turn a messy interior into an organised one and can be a focal point to boot.

- Buy special holders for your magazines. This makes for easy reference and a tidy display.
- Make the most of your filing cabinets: sandblast old ones or spray-paint them in a bright colour.
- Invest in shelves with doors, or hang drapes in front of them, so you can't see your clutter.
- Stash all office sundries (paper clips, pens, etc.) in boxes or baskets so your desktop is clear.

Bathrooms

- Conceal your lotions and potions in a cupboard or a basket to avoid a messy medley of bottles.
- For extra storage space, invest in a shower curtain with pockets.
- If you are short of space, erect glass shelves against the window. These can accommodate clutter and give you privacy at the same time.
- Keep the sides of your bath clutter-free. Buy tiles with in-built soap dishes and use sucker hooks for hanging flannels and brushes.

Bedrooms

- Make sure you have enough hanging space. If you have no wardrobe, hide clothes rails behind a giant bed head or in an alcove concealed with a blind or fabric drape.
- Cover a wall with hooks and hang up bags for storing scarves, jewellery, etc.
- Put your shoes in labelled boxes or use hanging shoe storage to keep clutter off the floor.

"Let go of the past and live in the present." Dawna Walter

Positive purging. Cleansing your home in this way is liberating on many levels. There is no getting away from the fact that clutter can have a deep, negative effect on us and removing it improves our mental well-being considerably. The more material things we have, the more we feel weighed down and hemmed in both emotionally and stylistically. People define us by our surroundings and our possessions and discarding the things we don't like allows us the freedom to reclaim ourselves, with the added benefit of a cleaner, less cluttered home.

Live only with what you love. The corollary of 'don't live with what you don't love' is also worth adhering to. It might sound obvious but it is easy to

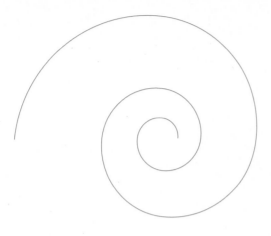

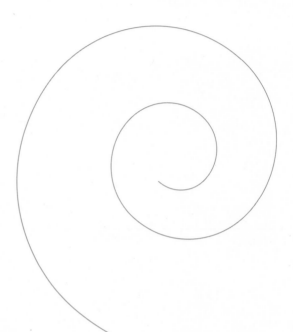

neglect this principle in the rush to furnish a home. How often have you bought furniture and objects that will 'do' because you can't find or afford exactly what you want, and ended up living with them well past their sell-by date? Resist the temptation to kit out your home instantly; living without something for a couple of months is infinitely preferable to living with a purchase you will regret for years. What's more, when you finally bring home the perfect bed or dining table, you will find that the wait will have been more than worth it.

Storage Is The Great Solution

If your home is more cluttered than most, don't give up on the paring-down process before you begin. It's important to realize that clutter is common to everyone; it is what you do with it that counts. The owners of those aspirational, near-empty interiors

you read about are not a breed apart, a race of ascetic people who live life without things (well, generally speaking that is). They have clobber like the rest of us, but – and here is the trick – they conceal it. Those sleek and streamlined rooms would look very different were it not for the fact that hidden behind their unadulterated façades lie countless, clutter-filled cupboards.

Storage may not be the sexiest of household amenities but it is the most essential if your aim is to create an organized and flexible living space, particularly if you are somebody who finds it difficult to throw things away. And it is reassuring to realize that we don't have to discard all our bits and pieces in the pursuit of a stylish modern home; we simply have to equip our interiors with adequate amounts of hiding space so that anything we don't want on show can easily be kept out of sight.

Storage options. Storage comes in many shapes and sizes. It can be built into the structure of your home in the form of cupboards, under-floor or above-ceiling space, so if you are buying a new-build home or adapting your existing interior, make sure that more storage space than you think you need is included in the plans. This kind of invisible storage makes it far easier to keep your interior uncluttered and it won't intrude on the space in the same way as free-standing furniture.

If you have little or no built-in storage, buy pieces of furniture with secret space for hiding things: a bench with a hollow seat; a cube-shaped coffee table; a bed with hidden drawers. Even by making maximum use of smaller scale storage solutions – boxes, baskets, hooks, for example – you can quickly transform a messy interior into an organized one.

Storage

The storage room. If you have a large house and a lot of possessions, allot yourself a storage room (or use a loft or cellar) for furniture and objects which you don't, for the moment, want on show but which can easily be brought out again. Alternatively, rent out-of-house storage space for a more permanent de-cluttering solution.

Hiding some of your things away gives you the flexibility to rationalize what you display and alternate your possessions month by month or even week by week, just as a gallery might circulate an extensive art collection. By emptying your home like this, you also clear the way for a brand new interior aesthetic. 'It's like having a blank piece of paper ready for the next bout of creativity,' says stylist Carolyn Quartermaine.

The Big Idea

Paring down your interior is one way of simplifying it, but there is another that can work just as well. Rather than simplifying your space by taking things out of it; you can do it decoratively by making all the elements in a room or even a whole house work towards one big idea. This idea or decorative concept could be anything from imposing a period look on a living space to choosing a monochromatic colour scheme; anything, that is, that will bind the disparate elements of a home together.

When creating an interior from scratch, stylists approach decoration in this way as a matter of course. Magazine features – even simple product-based 'shopping' stories – are generally pinned on a

central idea and a stylist is commissioned by concept, whether it's a period theme (a 50s-style living room, for example); an intellectual idea ('the home as comfort zone', for instance) or something purely sensual (a story based on colour or texture, perhaps). A stylist is thus programmed to produce room sets within tight conceptual parameters, with results that are visually very cohesive. These created interiors may not be 'real' but there is much we can learn from adopting a similarly focused approach to the decoration of our own homes.

Giving a room a 'look' makes decoration easier. Once you have established that you would like to have, say, a Moroccan bathroom, you have a direction in which to work. Do some research by looking through books and magazines and it will become

"Think of a room as a blank canvas; become inspired and begin."

Kelly Hoppen

An interior can be carried by one big idea.
Here a giant Buddha was the starting point
for a simple but decorative Oriental look.

clear what you will need. Working to a theme in this way will give you the confidence to be bolder than you might have been, safe in the knowledge that sticking to one style will give you a unified result.

Themes

The idea of a 'themed' interior might initially conjure up images of second-rate restaurants, but giving your decoration a bit of subject matter could be just what it needs. Don't feel you have to make a grand statement. You are trying to simplify your interior, after all, so pick an idea that will bring unity to your home without overcomplicating it. Opt for a theme you have your heart in and don't go over the top. Remember, you are trying to create a home not a theme park. Take into account your existing furniture and try to choose a concept that will work with it.

Also, make sure before you begin that your theme will be easy to execute and practical to live with.

Take inspiration from the things around you; the location of your home or simply its style could suggest a suitable decorative concept. If you've moved into a city loft space, for example, you might decide on an industrial look; if you live in a converted school, you might go for blackboard paint and simple wooden furniture. Adopt a style that seems integral to your surroundings rather than superimposed and keep away from purposely themed products which can be naff and unsubtle. If you want a nautical look in your cottage by the coast, steer clear of shell lampbases and starfish towels and go for 'grass roots' accessories – sea salvage, pebbles, driftwood – instead. This way you will get a look that has integrity and one that lasts.

Modern Romance

A stylish home doesn't need to be minimal and modern. Here, a collection of vintage fabrics, contemporary floral prints and decorative accessories make for an eclectic but unified bedroom. Even a row of colourful silk shoes fit the look.

Filling your home with furniture which is in keeping
with the period of the property can work brilliantly and
needn't be dull. Here an expansive living room in a
modernist house has been kitted out with classic
mid-century pieces which suit it perfectly.

Mid-century Modern

Your theme does not need to be in keeping with its location, of course; you could just choose a look you like. Anything can provide inspiration – a holiday, a fashion show, a walk in the park. Nature is a rich source of ready-made themes and tried-and-tested colour combinations, so simply steal ideas from the world around you. Any theme with a strong visual idea around which you can build your interior will give you all the decorative focus you need.

The Period Look

The style conscious may mock traditionalists for sticking religiously to a décor that is in keeping with the period of their houses, but adherence to one historical style does make for a logical and unified interior. And, of course, a period look need not be traditional; the 20th century has provided many clearly defined styles. A retrospective look can also be used to great effect outside its context. For

example, 60s style can look fantastic in a modern flat, and a groovy 70s scheme can work brilliantly in a Georgian terrace. Indeed, by juxtaposing old with new in this way, you will prevent your interior from becoming a stagnant period piece and help to make it personal, relevant and alive.

Mid-century modern. Born in the 1930s, developed in the 1940s and refined in the 1950s

and beyond, this is a look that is as modern now as it was 70 years ago and an aesthetic that mixes brilliantly with design from later periods. The phrase describes the shapely, ergonomic furniture that was being mass-produced in the middle of the twentieth century (in Scandinavia and America, particularly) from cheap materials such as plywood. The names to watch out for are, amongst others, Alvar Aalto, Hans Wegner, Arne Jacobsen, Charles and Ray Eames and Eero Saarinen.

Original pieces by the big names now cost a small fortune, but the up side is that you don't need to buy much to make it work: just one fluid Eames chair will give your office the sleek mid-century look. Alternatively, fake it by investing in reproductions (usually but not always cheaper than second-hand originals) or contemporary pieces that share the same elegant, pared-down aesthetic.

The Fifties. The post-war era was a time of inventions and inventiveness. To get into the spirit of the period, think curves, colour and kitsch. Seek out some original 50s' kitchen kit such as fat pastel-coloured fridges with rounded corners, American diner-style chairs or spindly-legged tables with tinted melamine tops. For tableware, choose graphic and

The Fifties

The bonus of a 50s look is that it can be put together fairly inexpensively as just a few elements can give you the right flavour. To get into the spirit of the period, think curves, colour and kitsch, and scour second-hand shops for suitably 'tasteless' accessories, such as this row of flying ducks (left).

shapely ceramics (geometric patterns are
a plus), coloured aluminium or
Tupperware and supplement these
with kitsch cocktail-style glasses. For
the living room, track down one of
those blobby molecular magazine
racks (a celebration of science if
ever there was one), buy fabrics and
wallpapers with flat and graphic
geometric patterns and finish off with
furniture from the period.

A big bonus of the 50s' look is that
it can be put together fairly inexpensively –
just a few accessories can give you the right
flavour. It is also relatively easy to find authentic
pieces and good 50s'-style reproductions.
Specialists in the period are now common on both
sides of the Atlantic and more and more retailers
have started selling on the internet.

The Sixties. The pop era in art, music, fashion and design, the 60s were all about big colour and bold ideas. The introduction of new technology for plastics (particularly injection moulding) and foam turned the conventions of upholstered furniture on their head, leading to an altogether new kind of design. There were brilliant one-piece plastic chairs (such as those by Verner Panton), fluid and organic-shaped seats (like Pierre Paulin's tongue chair or his mushroom chair, shown here), inflatable PVC 'Blow' chairs by Zanotta, and blatantly exhibitionist pieces such as Studio 65's 'Bocca' sofa that resembled a huge pair of lips. These designs have become icons of the period along with a host of equally flamboyant

"Go for anything that is big on curves and colour."

pieces by designers such as Ettore Sottsass, Joe Columbo and Olivier Mourgue.

Many 60s' pieces are still in production so you can buy new. Alternatively, hunt down second-hand originals in antique markets and specialist shops (though these days they can fetch high prices) or get the flavour of the period by buying new furniture in graphic shapes, 'modern' materials and psychedelic colours.

Finish the 60s' look off with space-age futuristic accessories, such as a Lava Lamp, or anything that's big on curves and colour. You could flick through old design magazines for ideas or scour the internet for 60s sites (highlights of the first Habitat catalogue, for example, can be viewed on their website). Finally, if you can, invest in some pop art or op art; after all, it was the art world that started off the 60s' design revolution.

The Seventies. More relaxed and apolitical than the energized decade before it, the 70s were big on comfort and pleasure and engendered a design that reflected a new, more laid-back approach to life. To get the look, think lounge lizards and shag-pile carpet, floor cushions and bean bags.

Seventies colour was softer, too, knocked back from the lurid tones of the 60s to more muted, grungey shades of brown, beige and soft orange; and pattern moved from psychedelia to calmer, geometric designs. The hippy look was still hot in fashion and furnishing with flowers (particularly oversized ones) a favourite motif on everything from cushions to tableware. But alongside hippy chic

came a new, far glitzier aesthetic as disco fever began to take hold of popular culture. So, if you want a truly 70s' look, a glitter ball is a must.

How To Use Colour
The most useful unifying tool in the decorative world, colour can simplify any interior. The key to success is to keep your scheme simple; use too many colours too close together and you can dull the impact of each. Don't be afraid to be bold or unconventional. Many a grand decorating scheme has been let down by an uninspiring palette.

Using colour is the best way of stamping your personality on a space. Your scheme can be bold and blatant or subtle and sophisticated; it can be anything you want it to be. If you introduce a fashionable colour into your interior, it's also a good way of keeping your home up to date (for more on fashion, see Chapter Four) and remember, a colour scheme is relatively easy and inexpensive to change when you feel like something new.

Be bold. A simple colour scheme doesn't mean you have to stick to whites and creams. Look around you for inspiration and pick colours that appeal to you – whatever they are. The purple of a sweet wrapper; the green of an olive; the silvery blackness of a piece of coal. These days, there are so many paints and fabrics available, that your choice is almost limitless. Trial and error is a good philosophy.

If you aren't sure which colours to go for, paint squares of your preferred tones on a wall and buy swatches of different toned fabric, then live with them for a week or two to see which works best with the light and with your existing furnishings.

Colour schemes. Be imaginative and experiment with different tones in different places. Take a look at the colour wheel and follow its principles if you want a fail-safe scheme (colours from the same segment will always work together; two opposite colours will complement each other, and three equidistant colours will give a harmonious but more dramatic result). Most importantly, choose colours that feel right for you and make the most of your home.

Colour

A one-colour background will provide a clear, strong backdrop to any mix of furniture. so if you have an eclectic collection of possessions, a monotone scheme is a good starting point. Don't play safe. These days paint manufacturers can match almost any tone, so choose a colour that will surprise and excite.

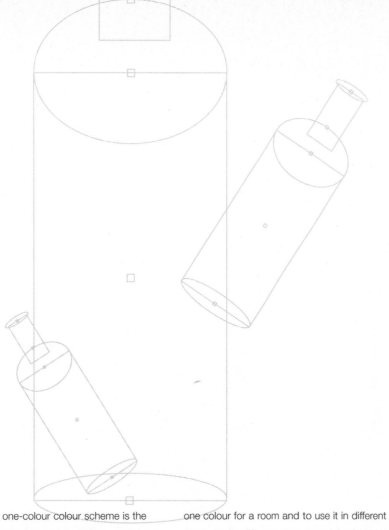

Monotone. The one-colour colour scheme is the most straightforward for a single room or even for a whole house and a plain background allows for more flexibility in furnishings. Choose a colour that complements your interior, but don't be conservative. A monotone scheme can take brilliant, unconventional colour in the right places – silver in the bathroom or pink in the kitchen, for example. Cover just one wall with colour or take it to the max by using the colour everywhere – walls, floors, furnishings and accessories. This blanket-of-colour effect is visually very striking and will give any room unity.

Using a chronology of colour. Another idea is to use a fading technique; or, in other words, to take one colour for a room and to use it in different strengths for different elements of the furnishing. Walls might be deep purple, for example; upholstery, in lilac and cushions and curtains, lavender or palest mauve. This 'chronology' of colour will give an intellectual edge to the room; bring together the disparate bits and pieces and look very groovy.

The bonus of a one-colour look. A monotone scheme gives you the freedom to mix different periods and styles of furniture. A Versailles-style chair reupholstered in lime green fabric looks good next to a modern coffee table in the same tone. Junk shop finds can be brought into line with a lick of the same-coloured paint or length of the same fabric.

Monotone

A different colour in every room. If you opt for a series of monotone schemes; in other words, a different colour in every room of the house, it is a good idea to choose tones from the same family of colours. Stylist Janie Jackson painted her house in an array of very pale pastel colours which gave an ethereal and very unified look to her living space and also made the most of the light (see page 17). Connect the rooms, if you like, by using one common accent colour in each to pick out details in each space, such as the picture rails or the skirting boards.

Two-tone

Using two colours will give you as graphic a result as a monotone look but more decorative flexibility – both in choice of colour and where to use it.

Colour combinations. If you decide to opt for two-tone in the structure of your interior (i.e. the walls, the floors and the ceilings), choose colours that work well together. That might sound obvious, but it is important to remember that these colours will provide the background to the rest of your furnishing and need to balance each other rather than jar. Strong colours can work well together – say fashionable companions such as sage green and purple or chalky blue and camel – and even clashing colours can offset each other brilliantly. Look abroad for ready-made colour combinations – the fuchsia and scarlet of Indian cloth, for example, or the pink and turquoise of a Mexican house. You might decide to use no colour at all, of course, and stick simply to black and white, a classic and dramatic combination that never seems to date.

Where to use them. Having two colours to work with gives you almost endless possibilities for the decoration of a room. You can use one shade for the structure of your space (i.e. for the walls, floors and ceilings) and another for the furnishing; you can make one colour dominant and introduce the other only as an accent in strategic places – at the back of an alcove, say, or on the inside of a cupboard door. This subtle two-tone effect can work brilliantly, particularly if you make the accent colour stronger than the dominant one, say a vivid purple or orange against a general eau-de-nil. Alternatively, you can make both colours work as hard as each other by painting two-tone patterns on a wall (in the form of stripes or even spots) or even by upholstering or painting your furniture in the alternate tones.

Two-tone

If you opt for a two-tone look, don't be tempted to stick to conservative co-ordinating shades. Strong and contrasting colours can work brilliantly together and should give you a more dramatic result. Look around you for tried-and-tested combinations – the blue and green of a cornflower, for example; the slate and ochre of the seashore; even the lurid orange and yellow of a carrier bag. Interspersed with panels of white, this fuchsia and red scheme (far left, top) is dramatic but not overpowering. A mix of soft brown and chalky blue (left and above) makes this interior the height of fashion.

Texture

How To Use Texture

Texture is something that, historically, most of us have taken for granted in the home. While carpets had to be soft and sofas comfortable, when it came to accessories or wall-coverings, visual impact was all that mattered. We would care about the look of a vase, but think little (consciously, at least) about how it felt in our hands. These days, things have changed. In today's uncluttered and streamlined interiors, the feel of things has taken on a new, more vital role. Indeed, if the style magazines are to be believed, texture has become the key element of today's homes, delivering an essential dose of sensuality to spaces that have often been stripped in the name of fashion of warmth and personality.

Filling your home with texture allows you to animate the interior without overcomplicating it; to keep it simple, without being bland – something that some bare, modern interiors are in danger of becoming. Even the simplest, most uncluttered space can feel warm and personal, and can (to adopt the jargon of interiors magazines) satisfy the soul, if filled with touchy-feely surfaces and objects.

Using contrasting textures. As a central decorative idea, using texture is a subtle one, but it can be very effective if it is done imaginatively. Think about creating contrasts: covering one wall with white pebble dash and the adjacent one with white gloss paint; putting a soft sheepskin rug next to coarse doormatting; a smooth ceramic vase against rough plaster. Consider the texture of everything you buy and try to pick materials and accessories with as much natural patina as possible (worn, grainy wooden boards for the floor, for example). Visitors may not immediately see why your home feels so good, but its impact should grow on them.

The one-texture look. With texture, as with colour, it's best to keep things simple and not to overdo it. Designer Andy Martin quoted in *Elle Decoration* advises: 'Use no more than three materials in any one room. It helps to keep the expression of the space focused.' For a single-minded approach, you could stick to just one texture for a room, or even for a whole house. A kitchen entirely kitted out in metallics, for example, will make an immediate impact (use aluminium or zinc as a cheaper alternative to stainless steel); a slate-clad shower-room will look sleek and sophisticated; a leather-lined office or hall will be both warm and functional, and look very cutting edge (though beware of the cost – leather flooring doesn't come cheap). Creating a homogenous, tactile background to a room in this way will give you a very cohesive result and allow you the freedom to be more eclectic with the accessories.

Quick Fixes

A pared-down uncluttered living space will give you bags of room to be creative. Here are four quick fixes that will give any interior an individual edge without overcomplicating it.

Festive Foliage

YOU WILL NEED

Dry leaves

Newspaper

Silver or gold spray paint

Fishing line

Scissors

Bulldog clips

Blu-tack or masking tape

Brilliantly simple and great for Christmas, these take no more than five minutes to make. Collect fallen leaves (the more interesting the shape the better), dry them and flatten overnight under a pile of books. Put the leaves on a large sheet of newspaper and spray with silver or gold spray paint. Leave to dry. Attach a piece of fishing line along the bottom of a mantelpiece or a shelf (using the Blu-tack or masking tape) and hang leaves at intervals from silver bulldog clips. Alternatively, stick the leaves to mirrors, doors, windows or walls.

➔ **Stylist tip.** Don't just use leaves. Spray twigs, pebbles, dried flowers or other found objects for an offbeat Christmas decoration.

YOU WILL NEED

Plain glasses

Tape or sticky labels

Frosting spray (available from most

   good DIY stores)

Graphic Glasses

1 Create a graphic pattern on the glass by attaching tape or sticky labels to those areas you want to keep clear.

2 Put tape over the top of the glass (to prevent spray from getting inside) and place it on a large sheet of newspaper. Then, gently spray the glass with the frosting spray. To prevent drips, it is best to build up a series of thin layers (letting the glass dry in between each) rather than one thick one. When the glass is frosted to the density you require, leave it to dry completely.

3 Carefully remove the sticky labels or tape to reveal the clear design.

➔ **Stylist tip.** Don't just stick to glasses. Transform plain bottles, vases and bowls in this way, too. You can even use frosting spray on a window to give you privacy without cutting out the light.

Pocket Calendar

"An easy and innovative way to keep yourself up to date."

YOU WILL NEED

A plastic CD holder with at least 31 pockets (these are available from high street stores and if you can't find one with enough pockets, buy several)
Stick-on letters or 'Letraset'

1 Create a calendar by sticking consecutive numbers onto the pockets of the CD holder from 1 to 31.

2 Attach the calendar to a wall or window with tape at the top or hang from string or wire, secured to the wall at either side.

➔ **Stylist tip**. Having a pocket for every day of the month means you can keep clutter at bay and yourself organised. Use the calendar for invites, notes, bills and reminders and have a monthly clear-out.

Named Napkin Rings

Idea from Rebecca Duke.

YOU WILL NEED

Napkin rings
Stick-on letters (from most good
art shops and stationers)

Simply stick your guest's name, initials or a
special message on his/her napkin ring for a table
setting with a difference.

→ **Stylist tip**. Get the napkin monogrammed
with a special message or even a photograph (try
photographic shops for this kind of service).

Display has always been an important part of interior decoration. In the past, items of furniture such as china cabinets, dressers and pedestals were designed specifically for this purpose – for showing off our best possessions; things that, in most cases, were there to be seen and not used.

In today's less formal and simpler homes, this kind of rarefied, self-conscious display seems anathema – partly because few of us have the requisite ornaments or the furniture on which to display them – and yet, paradoxically, the art of display is more relevant now than it has ever been.

Contemporary interiors are judged less on the value of their contents than on the way they look, and success does not come from buying in a quota of designer furniture (nice though that may be) but from displaying possessions effectively.

This democratic definition of style means that any of us can create a striking and sophisticated living space if – and here's the catch – we approach the decoration of our homes with imagination, individuality and an eye for detail.

The trick is to view our surroundings as a stylist might and to assess the visual impact of every element of the interior. It may not be easy to be objective about something so familiar, but try to stand back and really take stock of your home; to see it as others see it. In this way it should be easier to spot which areas need most work.

Don't just live with your possessions; look at them. Think about their shape, their form, their scale, and mix and match different objects to show each off to best advantage. Flick through design books and magazines and steal presentation ideas from the experts, and keep your eyes open for

displays that catch your eye in shops or travel brochures. Inspiration can come from anywhere. Consider every aspect of your house, not just the more obvious display areas such as a mantelpiece or tabletop. A graphic grouping of kitchen storage jars on a dresser shelf or a pile of brilliant lime-green towels on a purple bathroom stool can have just as much impact as a more obviously ornamental collection. Indeed, often the more mundane and unexpected the elements of a display, the more eye-catching it will be.

Mastering the art of display takes little time, little effort and no expense, but the results can be dramatic. Simply by adopting a few stylists' tricks – by playing with symmetry, scale or colour, for example, you can transform your home from a cluttered repository of possessions into a chic, contemporary living space.

Shape and Form

Don't neglect the less obvious parts of your home;
even an empty fireplace can become a striking
focal point if you treat it imaginatively.

"Show off the aesthetic qualities of every object."

Shape and Form

Before you begin a visual makeover of any room, think carefully about the form of the space itself. Is it expansive and open-plan or diminutive and cottagey? Is the room boxy or curved? What shape are the windows? The bare bones of an interior will often suggest how you should treat it, and how you can maximize the good points and minimize the bad.

If you are tackling a space which is fiercely rectilinear, for example, fill it with fluid furniture and curvy accessories and you will soften the feel of it considerably. If you are decorating an enormous warehouse conversion, emphasize its scale by displaying a row of identical chairs against a wall or by buying a giant bed or an oversized armchair. Use contrast, too, for dramatic effect: a sculptural 60s' sofa will bring instant vitality to a stately Georgian living room, decorative Louis XVI chairs add visual depth to any streamlined modern space.

Details count just as much as the grand scheme, so consider how to show off the aesthetic qualities of every object – no matter how mundane – to best effect. Group complementary shapes together (a row of plates or bowls along a mantelpiece or shelf, for example, or a cluster of cone-shaped candles on a table) or go for an arrangement of contrasting forms to surprise the eye. If you have few sculptural accessories, make graphic shapes with the display itself: a circle of pebbles on a floor, say, or a wavy line of nightlights on a tabletop. The simplest things, cleverly presented, can make the most impact.

Using Geometry

Geometry has been at the core of architecture, art and design for centuries, and its pure and ancient forms dominate all our homes. We live in geometric boxes; look out of geometric windows; use geometric furniture. The square, the circle, the rectangle, the triangle – shapes that can't be bettered in terms of pure design and graphic impact, but they are rarely exploited to their full potential in interiors. When you are trying to get your home visually into line, these provide an instant, fail-safe formula.

Display

When you come to style your interior, consider showing off the things you usually hide away. Taking an idea from the retail world, stylist Janie Jackson erected a series of clear Perspex rods to accommodate clothing in her bedroom (right). Hung with sleek wooden hangers, this open wardrobe is not only a feature in its own right, it also allows Jackson to make the most of her clothes; to display them by colour or texture, for example, for maximum visual impact.

Simple and graphic, geometrical shapes work naturally well together and, by emphasizing them, you can help to unify an eclectic interior. Play visual games with circles and squares to add interest to a room (see above and opposite, top) or use them simply to catch the eye, as with this wall painting (above right).

Circles and Squares

Make the most of what you've got. It's easy to ignore the geometrical shapes you have around you because they are so integral to the home, but if you draw attention to them, even exaggerate them with clever decoration or furnishings, you can create brilliant graphic effects.

Emphasize the shape of a square fireplace, for example, by painting or tiling the inside in a colour which contrasts with the rest of the room. Then, echo its shape in the surrounding display by placing tall oblong vessels on either side of the hearth, a square vase in the grate; a row of cube-shaped ceramics on the mantelpiece. By layering the geometric imagery in this way, you will achieve a strong look that's clean and graphic but not overdone. With a little thought, you can turn even the structural idiosyncrasies of your home into striking decorative conceits. In a loft space, for example, highlight the triangle of a pitched roof by treating it differently from the rest – by exposing the brickwork or by using an alternative paint finish.

Clever cut-outs. If you have few existing features with which to work, create your own. Get a builder to make you a simple square or a rectangular fireplace to give a central focus to a room or simplify the shape of an over-elaborate one by boxing it in with plywood or board. For a bolder statement, consider cutting a circular hole or a series of squares in an internal wall. On a practical level, this will link one room with the next and let in the light. Visually, it will look as dramatic as a piece of art, giving you framed views of the room next door.

This cut-out effect can work on a small scale, too. Replacing cupboard door handles and drawer pulls with simple circular holes will give any space a sleek modern edge (use a fret saw if you think you can tackle the job yourself, or commission a professional fret cutter). Similarly, a blind studded

with holes will give your windows a contemporary look and also cast wonderfully geometric patterns of light on the floor (if you do it yourself, make sure you use a fabric which won't fray). And why not take the peephole look to the limit by buying a couple of plastic Polo chairs by Robin Day – a 60s' design classic that still looks cutting-edge today.

Stick-ons. If you don't want to cut shapes out of your interior, do the opposite and add geometric details. Instead of making do with heavy and sculptural block-fronted shelves (a carpenter can make some up for you using hidden fittings or cover existing shelves with strips of MDF or plywood).

Alternatively, attach a series of boxes (square, oblong, circular, triangular – whatever appeals) to a wall. Place them at random for a freehand effect or at regular intervals for a more structured look, and think about introducing novel and eye-catching colour combinations. By adding an extra dimension to a room, these become mini geometric sculptures and look just as striking empty or full.

All circles and squares. For a truly cohesive result, take a geometrical theme right across your interior, from the very structure of a room to its furniture, furnishings and accessories. Try not to be too rectilinear; think about balancing lines with curves.

Geometric Details

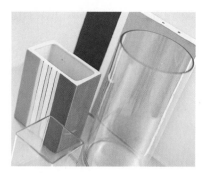

Using plaster and plywood, stylist Christina Wilson converted an unused fireplace into a display space (left) and, with a clever play on geometrical shapes, she made it more of an installation than anything purely practical. Geometrical displays (above) can work on a small scale, too.

"Adding the odd curvy surface to your home can have massive visual impact."

If you are decorating a square room with a square fireplace, for example, soften the boxy look with a circular rug, a circular mirror and a round coffee table. Feel free to go for the unexpected – say a triangular chest of drawers or a cylindrical chair – but remember to keep it simple to stop your scheme looking complicated and over-designed.

Be artistic. Take inspiration from the art world and create your own graphic geometric paintings and sculptures to give a room the ultimate finishing touch. Using a circular stencil, paint Damien Hirst-style spots on a wall or try your hand at Mondrian-inspired block painting. Alternatively, create your own in-house installation after artist Richard Long:

an arc of pebbles across a floor, perhaps, or a circle of candles on a table. It doesn't matter how mundane your materials: this kind of simple, geometric display will have great visual impact.

Going Organic
If you want a looser, less controlled interior scheme, give a more organic outline to your interior by introducing fluid forms and the kind of sculptural, amorphous shapes found in nature.

In the past, the organic aesthetic has been used to great effect in the home, particularly in the 60s as a contrast to the hard-lined, masculine feel of functional Bauhaus design. It couldn't have been more different. Organic shapes are not

Going Organic

Our homes are biased towards the linear, so adding the odd curved surface can make a massive impact. Freeform elements, such as this sinuous stainless steel worktop (left) will give any streamlined space a fluid feel, while curvy furniture and accessories (right and above) will add organic looks in an instant.

academic; they are gentle, elemental and feminine; and, as such, they can do much to soften any contemporary living space and give it soul. Naturally sculptural, they should also give as graphic a look to an interior as any more rectilinear scheme. Look to the art world for ideas. Browse through books on modern sculpture and take inspiration from the work of Henry Moore, Constantin Brancusi and Barbara Hepworth. Many modern retailers have in fact done just that and it's fairly easy to find designs for the home be it lampbases, candles or even items of furniture that are direct descendants of their sculptures.

Space-age style. Get a feel for the 60s' take on organic design by looking through magazines or specialist websites. Much of the freeform furniture designed at the time is still made today and many of the curvy accessories of the Space Age period, such as the Lava Lamp, are now design classics.

The great outdoors. Finally, and most simply, look around you. The natural world is full of organic shapes which have provided inspiration to the most recherché artists and designers. The rounded pebbles on a beach, a plump squash, the curve of a flame or leaf. Any combination of these fluid forms should give you an interior that is at once comfortable and modern.

Keep the furniture soft. If you are a Feng Shui aficionado, you'll know that soft-edged furniture will bring good *chi* (energy) to a living space, curvy shapes will give you an interior which is informal and easy on the eye. There are lots of 'organic' pieces to choose from at both ends of the price scale, from classic and expensive designs such as Arne Jacobsen's egg-shaped armchair, down to cheaper, more accessible products such as the amorphous go-anywhere bean bag. Fluid furniture, too, is on the increase. Inspired by the curvy plastic

chairs of the 60s, contemporary designers are bringing out sculptural one-piece designs in all manner of materials. One of the best is the ingenious 'Bookworm' shelving system by Ron Arad, (see page 25).

Be bulbous. Whether you are going for an all-out-organic look or simply want to offset the rectilinear feel of a room, plump and sculptural accessories are a must. Opting for kidney-shaped plates and dishes, for example, will make your tabletop a talking point; choosing a door-knob with a curve will instantly transform a dull door. If you can't buy what you need, improvise. Get a gourd electrified to make an ingenious organic lampbase or use an artist's palette for displaying fruit.

Why curves work. By adding organic elements to your interior in strategic places, you can give a graphic edge to a room without making it look tight

"A play on scale is often at the heart of a successful visual idea."

or over-designed. The key to success, as always, is to keep it simple. Stick to natural shapes as much as you can and don't go over the top: an excess of curvy details can spoil the subtlety of a decorative scheme.

The Size Issue

Playing With Scale

Scale is something we might think about when we are buying a house, but rarely consider when it comes to decoration or display. This is a mistake. Furnishing with a sense of scale can transform an interior, allowing you to play visual tricks with proportion and also add dramatic impact to even the smallest displays.

Whether you decide to enlarge or shrink certain key elements of a room or simply group your possessions with an eye to their size, look around for inspiration. Consider the use of oversized and undersized objects in public displays – in shop windows and galleries, for example, or in film and theatre sets where a play on scale is often at the heart of a successful visual idea. And don't take the thing too seriously: the best schemes are those with a good dose of wit.

Descending and ascending scale. In a small space, illustrate a sense of scale literally by displaying a collection of similar or even identical objects in order of size. Use families of furniture – a nest of tables, for example – which can also be stacked up together when you need more room.

In a large space, show an unexpectedly large collection of objects to accentuate the size of the place. Hang a series of pictures along a wall,

Playing with scale is an easy and effective way to make any display eye-catching. Families of furniture, such as the nest of tables shown here, will make it easy for you, but by grouping any objects according to their size you can create a graphic visual effect.

The Size Issue

"Big objects can make a big impact."

graduating from the very big to the very small, or display a selection of natural found objects (such as stones or leaves) in ascending size order along a shelf or across a table. Think, too, about using this expanding technique vertically as well as horizontally by stacking increasingly small boxes on top of each other, perhaps.

Undersize
We are not talking about miniature figurines or dolls' house furniture here: tiny things needn't be twee. Arrangements of undersized objects can be graphic and eye-catching if they are surprising and imaginative; and, on a practical level, they can make a small room seem bigger.

Use a small-scale concept in picture display, for example. Place a tiny painting in a large surround or frame a series of mini pictures. A succession of small things will make a big visual impact. Be inspired by artists such as Antony Gormely, who created a room full of mini figurative sculptures for his *Field* installation, and group a collection of small objects along a shelf, in a glass-topped table or in a neglected corner of a room. Anything can work, so use whatever you have to hand: glass bottles, perhaps, or even jewellery.

Oversize
Using overscaled objects in the home appeals to the child in all of us. There is something nostalgic and comforting about being dwarfed by familiar things. Being swallowed up in an enormous floor cushion or perching on a giant bed, for example, takes us right back to the fairy tales of the nursery. Aside from the emotional impact of the oversized, giant furniture and objects can also transform an interior both visually and practically. Overscaled elements work best in isolation, so if you choose to play with scale in this way, don't go too far. An unexpectedly large lampshade, for example, will make a grand and graphic statement in any room; an enormous solitary sofa in a minimal open-plan home will accentuate the dimensions of the place, define the space it sits in and – most importantly – will accommodate lots of people.

The Graphic Solution
Big things, of course, cost big money, but there are cheaper ways of using an overblown conceit which are just as effective. One of the best and most graphic techniques is to use enlarged type or

Playing with Scale

Just one giant object in an interior will provide all the impact you need.

Balance

imagery on a wall or floor. This can be done relatively easily and the results can be dramatic. One giant letter, a scaled-up stencil or an overblown line of poetry painted on a wall will give an innovative edge to any interior.

Keep it Even

Symmetry

The human notion of beauty is closely linked with symmetry. In the visual world, we respond to equilibrium and reflection, to a certain regularity of form; and symmetrical structures and shapes have consequently been at the heart of architecture and design since classical times. Indeed, most of our homes still follow a symmetrical pattern both outside and in (a front door with a window on either side; a fireplace framed by twin alcoves, and so on) and

simply by making maximum use of this given framework, you can create a look which will be visually balanced and thus easy on the eye.

Look at the structure of your interior and decide where a symmetrical display would have most impact. If you have a niche on either side of a chimney breast, for example, draw attention to it by showing identical objects in each. Mirror-image displays can't help but work and they don't need to be complicated. Even a couple of matching vases will give you a strikingly graphic result.

Using pairs helps to ground an interior, to pin it down visually. As art director Ruth MacDonald explains: 'Once you have attempted to define symmetry within a room, then everything else can follow and can be as haphazard as you like.' So, if you have no symmetry in the structure of your interior, superimpose it by planting pairs of objects in

strategic places – on either side of a door or a window, perhaps, or on each side of a bed. And think about creating symmetrical displays on a smaller scale, too.

Asymmetry

Using symmetrical display in the home will give you a comfortable, classical and restrained look, so if you want something a little more edgy and off-kilter, consider its antithesis. Asymmetrical displays can be very effective if they are put together carefully and should give a more quirky and personal edge to an interior. First, think about off-setting those twin alcoves or carbon-copy side tables with displays of contrasting objects. Place different coloured blooms in your complementary vases or show giant ceramics on one side and tiny ones on the other. By undercutting what is expected in this way you will

"Once you have defined symmetry in a room, then everything else can be as haphazard as you like." Ruth Macdonald

instantly draw the eye. Asymmetrical displays, like asymmetrical objects, seem less self-conscious and less designed than their more balanced, more perfect, counterparts and adding a dose of spontaneity and irregularity to an interior can prevent it from looking sterile or overstyled.

Repetition
If you haven't got collections of sculptural ceramics or recherché designer objects to display, don't discard the concept altogether. The most mundane possessions can make just as much impact as any number of high-brow artefacts if they are grouped with imagination and an artistic eye. One of the most simple and most effective techniques to use is

repetition. Straightforward it may be, but a row of identical objects is hard to beat for graphic impact. If you are displaying small things, the key to success is numbers. While one can of baked beans will look like, well, a can of baked beans, fifty of them will look like an installation (really!). For larger objects, a group of three or five can be enough (but make sure to stick to an odd number to give the display a central focus).

Think about using repetition both horizontally and vertically in the home. A line of pictures or even strip lights, placed one on top of the other, will have an impact that a single one never could. Consider, too, adding a new dimension to a linear display by using gradations of colour. You could upholster a row of stools in varying tones of the same shade, for instance, or like Andy Warhol, you could buy or make artworks that repeat the same image in different colours along a wall.

Creating Pictures

We've talked about the principles of display, but where do you put them into practice? There are the obvious places, of course. Any room will have its quota of display areas – a mantelpiece, perhaps, or a central shelf – but when you are trying to create a visually strong, styled interior, it is equally important to think about the less obvious areas. Nowhere should be neglected.

Before you begin a visual makeover of any room, it is a good idea to empty it of clutter so that you can get a feel for the bare bones of the space. Every room will have its own structural

Repetition

idiosyncrasies, so consider how you want to treat these before you begin on the details. In the sitting room, for example, there may be an unsightly alcove that needs to be concealed or a fireplace that needs attention. Clever display can draw the eye towards the good features of a room and away from the bad, and the individual needs of a space will often dictate where you should begin.

Don't be too ambitious at the start. Address the most obvious display areas first and think how you can set each off to best advantage. What the stylist is so good at is creating pictures – or striking focal points in strategic places, so think how you can do the same. Try out different kinds of display to see which looks best throughout your interior and pick up a camera to view the results of your work just as a stylist would. In this way you will get a very focused impression of its visual impact.

Remember that dramatic display is as much about what to leave out as what to put in, so don't be tempted to fill your room with objects. You may find that simply by removing the clutter you will have transformed a nondescript alcove into an eye-catching feature.

Areas of Display

The Alcove

This is perhaps the most obvious display area in the home, but it often gets neglected. We stuff our alcoves with shelves full of books and videos, with little thought about what they look like; we use them to store stereo equipment and televisions without considering just how unattractive the result will be. An alcove can be the decorative focus of a room and, as a self-contained storage space, it's a brilliant place to show off your possessions. By simply

Fresh Focus

Take inspiration from the stylist and arrange
everything in a room – from the furniture down to
the smallest accessory – with a view to its visual
impact. Simply by learning the art of effective
presentation, you can transform your interior
in an instant.

"As a self-contained storage space, an alcove is a brilliant place to show off your possessions."

rethinking the way you treat it, you can do much to transform the look of an interior.

There are many ways to make an alcove – whatever its shape catch the eye. If space is at a premium and you need to use niches for storing books, try to arrange them aesthetically – by the colour of the covers, perhaps, or at least by size. It may go against the intellectual grain to think about the look of your books but they make a strong visual impact if they are cleverly and tidily arranged.

If you have the shelves but few books to fill them with, use alcoves to display collections of similar objects. Don't be conservative; unexpected things will grab the attention more than carriage clocks and china figurines – a collection of old irons, perhaps, or, at Christmas, rows of sprayed silver leaves held in postcard clips. If you choose, instead, to display just a few objects, think about the shape and the scale of the space and pick things that will stand out, complement each other and work well against the background colour of the room.

For those with few possessions, there is another option: display just one dynamic object or even leave alcoves empty. Treat the space imaginatively by painting it a colour which contrasts with the rest of the room, for example, or by flooding it with coloured light, and it will become an instant and compelling decorative feature.

The Mantelpiece

So often obscured with out-of-date invitations and dusty family photographs, the mantelpiece is ripe for transformation in most households. As a feature, it is there to be looked at and can carry strong visual ideas which can lift the rest of the room. Browse through your possessions and decide which would work best on the mantelpiece; try different arrangements of objects, plants or even books.

Mantelpiece displays don't need to be complicated; the simplest ideas are the most successful. A mantelpiece bare but for two curvy pots in toning colours will look graphic and modern; single bold blooms in a row of identical vases more

Alcoves

The alcove is one of the most obvious display spaces, so don't fill it with unsightly clutter (left). Use it to show off eye-catching or unexpected objects, as here, or – for a graphic effect – paint the recesses in contrasting colours.

striking than a blowsy bunch. For a display which is a little more substantial, think about the look of the mantelpiece as a whole rather than concentrating on the individual elements, so that you choose objects that work well together. Play with symmetry, shape and colour to create a mini work of art.

Tips for Transforming your Mantelpiece

● Change your display frequently to keep your interior alive and come up with seasonal themes for special occasions.
● Repetition works brilliantly, so line up whatever you have to hand, whether postcards, starfish or colourful tiles.

● Surprise the eye by using your mantelpiece as a bookshelf for good-looking books and find dramatic bookends to complete the picture.
● Get those invitations in order. Stuff them into a silver toast-rack for an instant sculpture or stack them up like a house of cards.
● Think about offsetting the linear look with some curves: a sculptural ceramic vase (with or without the flowers), a series of circular pictures or some wavy candles.
● If you have nothing above your mantelpiece, make the most of the space by including unexpectedly tall objects in your display for maximum impact.
● Colour co-ordinate your displays.

● Line up ornate empty picture frames (find old gilt ones in markets and junk shops or make your own using plaster or plastic ceiling cornice).
● Make a light-show out of your mantelpiece by topping it with a row of candles or nightlights (see quick fix on page 104); by draping it with fairy lights or by using it to show off a designer light box for an innovative display.

The Fireplace
We often focus on the mantelpiece at the expense of what is beneath it. A fireplace, too, makes a good display area, whether or not it is in use. If it is, your potential for display will be limited but, if you have a

Mantelpiece Make-overs

The mantelpiece is the main focus of a room, so maximise its potential by abandoning clutter in favour of graphic and eye-catching arrangements of objects. Give your mantelpiece a seasonal theme, if you like – silver leaves and pebbles for Christmas, for example – (opposite, left) or stick to a monochromatic colour scheme (opposite, centre). And if you want to bring a bit of nature inside, be creative. Instead of customary bunches of flowers, line up a row of single blooms (opposite, right) or incorporate fruits and grasses into the mix for a dynamic, offbeat display.

"Edit clutter to create a more restful ambience." Tricia Guild

real fire, try to keep the hearth tidy and interesting by filling it with cone-shaped firelighters or graphically arranged wood blocks when it is not lit. If you have a gas fire which fills the space, consider the surrounding areas and draw the eye away from the fire itself by placing interesting objects on either side of the grate: perhaps a couple of sculptural plants (beware they don't dry out), some shapely vases or even a pair of decorative shoes.

If all you have is a hole in the wall, make it a focal point by filling it with ingenious and colourful displays. Flowers are an obvious choice (keep them big and graphic), but there are countless other alternatives. You could pack the space full of logs (see page 55), or books; use it to show off a collection of tribal art or sculpture; even, if it's big enough, fill it with colourful cushions to make a self-contained seating area.

Alternatively, go for a more decorative solution.

Paint the inside of the chimney breast in a colour which contrasts with the surrounding wall, or cover it with shells or a patchwork of brilliant tiles. As an isolated detail in the room, the fireplace can get away with dramatic decoration, even if the rest of the interior is calm and understated.

The Furniture

While traditional display furniture, such as the china cabinet, may look out of place in today's pared down interior, its function is a valid one. Having somewhere to place and show off your possessions makes styling an interior far easier. So, if your home lacks integral presentation space (mantelpieces and alcoves et al), think about investing in modern furniture that fulfils the same role.

Choose go-anywhere pieces, such as a sleek wooden console table which will look just as good in a bedroom or a living room and which can be used

Fireplaces

Often the simplest ideas are the most successful.
A mantelpiece bare but for two curvy ceramics in
toning colours will look graphic and modern; a single
bold bloom in a row of identical vases, more than a
blowsy bunch.

for displaying all manner of objects. In an open-plan room, invest in a bookshelf-cum-room-divider which will give you plenty of cubby holes for magazines, vases or pieces of sculpture; or opt for a screen with slots for displaying photographs or pictures.

And don't forget to make the most of the furniture you have. Use the back of a sofa to display a beautiful length of fabric; the front for an array of interesting cushions. Use the end of a bed to show off an embroidered shawl; the edge of the bath for a row of votive candles. Stylist Kate Constable even topped the seats of her chairs with little set pieces of her favourite possessions. With a little thought,

and imagination you can turn almost every part of your home into a display space.

The Bathroom

Unlike that other functional area – the kitchen, the bathroom is a private space and it rarely gets the visual overhaul it often sorely needs. Cluttered with cleansing paraphernalia, even the cleanest bathroom can look unappealing, so think how you can give yours a revamp. The same theory applies here as elsewhere: use simple presentation tricks to make the most of the space and of its contents. Transfer lotions and potions into good-looking glass bottles,

for example; stash sponges and flannels into bowls or baskets; keep the surfaces clear. With a little thought, it is easy to transform this functional space into a sensual and stylish haven.

The Walls

Most of us, of course, do use the wall for display, but our use of it tends to be very limited. We may put up pictures or photographs; we may hang up the odd antique textile, but there is so much more we can do to maximize its visual potential.

An unused wall is the perfect place to show off idiosyncratic collections of objects. Erect a series of

Bathroom Display

You may not think of the bathroom as an area for display, but by arranging its contents with a creative eye, you can transform it from a dull utility space into a stylish and inviting haven. Conceal all the necessary clutter in cupboards, boxes or baskets and eliminate fussy furnishings. Simply by substituting a tatty blind for sleek frosted glass at the window (top left), you can do much to update the space. In a modern take on the natural look (left and far left, top) stylist Christina Wilson displays books and bottles on heavy wooden shelves in her chic urban bathroom.

mini shelves for displaying anything from tin toys to old clocks, or cover a wall with hooks from floor to ceiling and hang up handbags (which will also give you additional storage space), old keys or even – in a utility space – bits and pieces that you are always losing (scissors, a ball of string, a can opener). Even very mundane objects can grab the attention if they are displayed imaginatively.

Think, too, about using your walls as a canvas on which to experiment with more graphic visual ideas. Paint one or a series of panels (oblong, square – whatever shape you like) in a colour which contrasts with the general tone of the room, or do your own spot painting (see right – all you'll need is a plumb-line and a compass or circular stencil). If you haven't the money to buy in works of art, painting directly on the wall like this is a brilliant way of creating your own and, it can be changed easily and cheaply, whenever you feel like it.

Innovative Ideas for Picture Display

● If you have a picture rail, hang art from chains (in whatever finish appeals), ribbon or rope.

● Look out for interestingly shaped frames: the odd circular image can make all the difference.

● Place a sequence of pictures in one giant frame (overlap the images or use a multi-aperture frame for a more structured look).

● Stick a single line of postcards right around the room for a graphic band of art.

● Display your favourite postcards or cuttings in transparent plastic CD holders and hang them in a series.

The Floor

We strip it down, we cover it up, but we rarely maximize the floor's potential as a display space. If your interior is on the plain side, why not liven it up by making a bold statement underfoot? There are countless different flooring materials available these days, so be adventurous and consider unexpected textures or eye-catching colour combinations.

Walls

Get creative with your walls. Cover them with wooden slats for a rustic look; hang them with fabric drapes for something more sophisticated; or – for the ultimate grand gesture – copy and enlarge a print of an old master and use that as wallpaper (opposite). This page: echoing the shape of the adjacent clocks, this spot-painted wall is offbeat and eye-catching.

Floors and Ceilings

Transform an uninspiring kitchen by designing your own vinyl floor (it will cost you but you will get an original bespoke result). Spruce up a bland bathroom with a chequerboard of brilliant rubber tiles, a textural pebble floor or even a glass one (be prepared to pay for the privilege). Whatever you decide to do, make sure at the start that your chosen material will work in the required space by getting advice from the experts and, if you are not a flooring aficionado, get it laid professionally.

Even in rooms where you have plain carpet or natural flooring, you can add a bit of vitality with rugs and runners. Today, it is relatively easy to find designs which are bold and graphic, so choose one that will complement the interior both in shape and colour (a curvy rug for example, will soften a rectilinear space; see 'Going Organic', page 64).

Alternatively, make patterns with the carpet itself. Lay two or more different colours in one room – in wide stripes, perhaps, or in a spot effect like stepping stones. If you are prepared to pay a bit extra for your floor, almost anything is possible.

The most straightforward way to decorate your floor, of course, is to paint it. Don't feel you have to stick to whitewash or wood stain; cover a floor with graphic patterns or even pictures to give it a creative edge. One stylist covered all the floors in her house to great effect with intricate Moorish-style designs.

Aside from the flooring itself, there are many other ways you can up the impact of your floor. Use the edges to display a row of pictures or a collection of pottery; the corners to show off unexpected groups of found objects – a pile of pebbles perhaps, or a pool of clean, white gravel.

You could even create islands of display across the main sweep of the floor to break the space up visually.

The Ceiling

The ceiling can do more than simply accommodate the lights. It can become the main feature of a room and you don't need to be Michelangelo to make it have an impact. Why not paint the ceiling in an unexpected colour; cover it with wallpaper; even – if you are living in a loft space – cut a hole (or a series of holes) in it so you can see the sky. And use it as a display space, too. At Christmas, hang baubles from beams or the ceiling itself (using masking tape or Blu-tack, which shouldn't lift the paint) or invest in a few graphic mobiles (look to Alexander Calder for inspiration) which will fill your interior with aerial art.

Using Flowers

Flowers have always been used in the home. They bring colour, life and a touch of sensuality to the blandest of living spaces. A floral display can transform a room instantly and relatively cheaply, whether it is a colourful bunch or a single sculptural stem and, while it has become fashionable recently to display vases without the flowers, they still have a vital role to play in contemporary interiors.

Think carefully about what flowers you choose and approach their arrangement imaginatively. Consider their colour, their shape and their texture and dream up innovative ways to show them off around the house. Remember, the simplest of displays can be the most successful.

Playing with colour

Think decoratively about the flowers you buy and choose tones that will make an impact in your interior. For wrap-around colour, go for a monotone display that co-ordinates with the surroundings. This will give a room a seamless, sophisticated air and it needn't be dull if your colours are bold or off-beat (deep purple, perhaps, or all green). Alternatively, pick a tone for your flowers that will contrast dynamically with the colour of the interior. A bunch of red roses against a fuchsia pink wall, for example, will look brilliantly kitsch; orange marigolds or tulips against lime, fresh and modern.

Think, too, about the dynamics of the floral display itself. You could buy a selection of different flowers in the same colour, or go for a multi-

Using Flowers

"Even a bunch of weeds can make an impact."

coloured display of the same bloom. Even a bunch of six clashing gerberas in a simple vase will transform a dull alcove into a brilliant one.

Playing with Shape

These days it is fairly easy to get hold of exotic flowers with dramatic shapes. They may be expensive but even one or two blooms can change the personality of a room in an instant. Look around to see what inspires you – the globe of an allium, the cone of a lupin or the linear structure of a bunch of bamboo, and flick through a book on ikebana to get a feel of how you might structure your arrangement. Mix and match different shapes or

display just one giant and graphic bloom. The appeal of some flowers will come and go, but here are some shapely classics:

Top Ten Sculptural Blooms

- Peony: curvaceous, old-fashioned and perfect for a vintage look.
- Allium: sculpture on a stem. Go for the biggest for a bold, modern impact.
- Orchid: weird, exotic, great for an Eastern look.
- Dahlia: star-like, colourful, a go-anywhere classic.
- Poppy: down to earth and naturally elegant.
- Iris: cool and sculptural.
- Shamrock: green, spiky and interesting.

- Lily: the shapely classic. To avoid cliché, go for unusual varieties in deep, unexpected colours.
- Tulip: ubiquitous but hard to beat for curves.
- Gerbera: a bit of a style cliché but brilliant for an informal and colourful display.

Why not experiment with different flowers each week, and don't forget that some of the simplest are the most shapely. The shamrock (a member of the chrysanthemum family), for example, will bring an unusual edge to any display; the tulip and the poppy are hard to beat for graphic curves. Even a bunch of weeds can make an impact if you pick them for looks and display them imaginatively.

Display ideas. Think up innovative ways to display your flowers. To make a change from vases, use unexpected containers such as old plastic or milk bottles (see the Quick Fix on page 133), test tubes or plain drinking glasses. Remember that water will magnify whatever is inside it, so see-through vessels can make for interesting visual effects.

Feel free to go for blowsy bunches (a jug full of wild meadow flowers will always look good), but consider, too, that single blooms can make more impact (and save you money). Look in magazines and books for ideas and try out alternative displays – a row of simple vases with a single peony in each, perhaps; or a few stems of snakegrass in a wavy wooden pot.

Consider, too, displaying only parts of flowers – dried heads sewn onto a muslin curtain; petals floating in a large flat bowl; leaves scattered across a tabletop. Such natural details can make a brilliant finishing touch to any interior.

And don't just stick to flowers

• Create displays using only foliage. Leaves and grasses come in graphic shapes and an all-green scheme can have bags of visual impact.

• Use fruit instead of flowers or mix the two. Limes, lemons and kumquats, for example, will bring a colourful, eccentric edge to a display.

• Mix stones (black pebbles or white gravel are particularly good) into your display to give it added visual interest (see page 91).

Natural Display

Flowers, key tools of the stylists' trade, can transform an interior instantly and inexpensively. When you buy, choose blooms in sculptural shapes or in colours which complement your interior. Think up innovative ways of displaying them; even a single flower in a simple vase or a giant leaf on a plate can make a massive impact.

Quick Fixes

Mastering the art of display needn't
be difficult or time-consuming. Here
are five inspired quick fix ideas to
show you just how easy it is.

Easy Picture Frames

YOU WILL NEED

2 sheets of bevelled-edge glass

Bulldog clip

Image (we used Polaroids and
   a Chinese paper cutting)

1 Choose your glass and get it
   cut to size.

2 Position your image between
   the two pieces of glass.

3 Fix in place with a bulldog clip
   (a sturdy clip can be used at
the bottom of the frame as a stand –
see above left).

→   **Stylist tip.** You can use any
transparent or translucent material as long as it
is stiff enough. And why stop at images? Display
leaves, stamps, material – or anything 2–D that
takes your fancy.

Idea from Vicky Barker

YOU WILL NEED

A selection of images
Hardboard
Spray adhesive
Spray varnish

 1 Take a selection of your favourite images – photographs, illustrations or drawings – and get them colour-copied and enlarged to the required size (most photographic shops offer this service).

2 Using spray adhesive, glue them onto pieces of hardboard or MDF (available from any DIY store) which have been cut to the same size (or slightly larger if you want to create a frame effect).

3 Finish with spray varnish (a few thin layers works better than one thick one) and simply prop on a shelf, a mantelpiece or even the floor.

➜ **Stylist tip.** Save time by simply laminating an image which will make it longer-lasting, too.

Idea from Emily Jewsbury.

Instant Art

"Turn your favourite cuttings into pictures you can display."

Personalised Notebooks

YOU WILL NEED

Notebook

Sticky-backed plastic

Scissors

1 Cut the plastic to size using the open notebook as a pattern and allowing for an extra 2cm (¾ in) around the edge.

2 Gently peel off the backing paper and lay the back of the book onto the right-hand half of the sticky plastic. Press down carefully to avoid air bubbles and then gently turn the book over onto the other half of the plastic to cover.

3 Open up the notebook; cut triangles of plastic off at each corner and snip off the excess at the ends of the spine. Stick overlaps to book cover and smooth with the back of your hand.*

*If the inside of the cover looks messy, stick a piece of coloured paper on top to hide the edges, or simply stick the first page of the notebook to the cover.

→ Stylist tip. Think of alternative coverings. Colourful felt, fashionable fabric, wallpaper or Chinese newspaper would be just as effective as plastic.

"Go back to school and jazz up boring notebooks with great new covers."

Idea from Amanda Smith at *Elle Decoration.*

Funky Mousemats

" Update your desktop
with the latest looks."

Simply get your favourite images – photos, post-cards, wallpaper designs – turned into a mousemat (try local photographic shops for this kind of service). Bespoke design has never cost so little.

→ **Stylist tip.** Do the same for table mats and coasters or even for bathroom tiles.

Spotlights

YOU WILL NEED

Transparent plastic or glass stand-up
   photo frame
Coloured plastic sheets (available from
   good stationers)
Nightlights

Simply slide a coloured plastic sheet into the frame
and stand the nightlight behind it for an instant,
colourful mantelpiece or shelf display.

"Transform dull
nightlights into a brilliant
and colourful display."

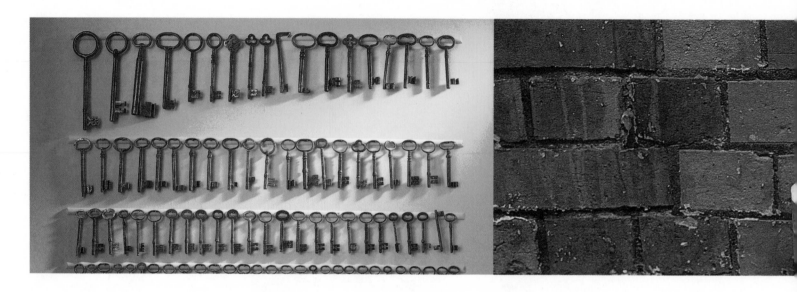

Lateral thinking lies at the root of any creative idea. The best innovations in art, design, science and technology are often the result of one person's capacity to view the world with fresh eyes and see beyond what is immediately in front of them; in other words, to side-step the obvious and the orthodox and come up with something entirely new.

A lateral approach can work in the home, too, and this is what the stylist is so good at. Of the interiors we see in magazines and on television, the most striking are not those that are expensively furnished and out of reach, but rather those that are full of ingenious and accessible ideas that can have an instant impact on our own homes.

So, when it comes to styling your own living space, don't rush out to buy the latest designer must-haves, look at your interior afresh and consider alternative ways of transforming it. Think about turning convention on its head by displaying very mundane things as if they were works of art. Think about using ordinary objects in extraordinary ways. Consider using the stylist's shopping list and sourcing furniture and materials that aren't traditionally found in the home – old office chairs, for example, or industrial aluminium flooring.

Take inspiration from everything around you, whether it's the shape of a shop sign or the texture of a theatre seat. By thinking laterally and playing with the context and the content of your interior, you will find that you can turn it quickly and cheaply into a chic, individual and eye-catching space.

One word of warning: don't go over the top with offbeat ideas or your interior may look too self-conscious and overstyled. You want to surprise the eye, but shock value is not what you are after.

Alternative Displays

Generally in our homes we show off the kind of things that people expect to be shown off – beautiful vases, paintings, flowers – but think of the alternatives. By using unconventional displays of unexpected objects, you can create a striking, individual interior that no one will forget in a hurry.

Everyday Sculpture

Be unconventional and display very mundane objects in the home. Place a collection of old cutlery on a wall, a row of milk bottles on a shelf – anything can work if it appeals to you. The key is to see the beauty in everything – the curve of a cup or the colour of a paper bag – and to be brave enough to show it off. What's more, you'll be in good company. The Dada artists were the first to treat everyday objects

Sculpture in the Everyday

Few of us think of displaying mundane things as if they were works of art but by treating the commonplace object as something that deserves to be looked at, it can't help but take on a new sculptural presence. Be inspired by the Dada and Pop artists and show off anything that appeals – whether it is a collection of old keys, some colourful jelly moulds or even a stack of toilet rolls (left). This is an approach that can be carried right around the house and while it may take an act of faith to put everyday items on a pedestal, such unconventional displays will grab attention and give your interior instant lateral looks.

as art. Marcel Duchamp's infamous *Fountain* (1917) put the urinal on a pedestal, while Kurt Schwitters used rubbish from the gutter in his paintings. Their work was iconoclastic and ironic, of course, but it had an enormous impact on the art world, influencing the Pop artists of the 1960s such as Andy Warhol and Richard Hamilton, who incorporated images from popular culture in their work to challenge the conventional notions of art. And conceptual artists today are still doing this: recently Tracey Emin, a contender for the Turner Prize, made an exhibition of her unmade bed at London's Tate Gallery.

Clever combinations. As well as thinking laterally about displaying your possessions, tap into newt design talent for furniture and objects which are quirky and unexpected. Scour shops, magazines and the internet for designs which play witty games with shape, form and material – a macraméd chair or a light made from milk bottles, for example.

Mix and match. Another way to bring a quirky feel to your home is to create unexpected combinations of furniture or objects. Try mixing the very grand with the very prosaic (a gilded chair on a raw concrete floor, say); the luxurious with the industrial (a lush velvet quilt on a scaffolding-pole bed); the very big with the very small (see 'Playing With Scale', page 68). Incorporating striking visual and textural contrasts into your interior will give it depth and interest.

Ordinary-Extraordinary

Using the Ordinary

For commonplace things to make an impact in the home, you don't have to display them in isolation as art. You can give a lateral spin to your interior in a more subtle way by using objects, furniture or materials out of context within the fabric of your decorative scheme.

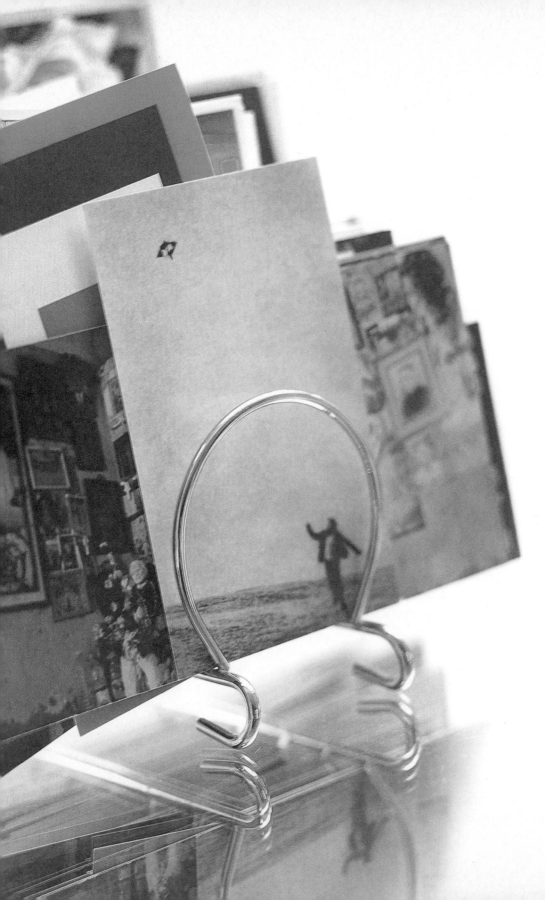

The key to the lateral approach is to see the beauty in everything – whether it is the curve of a cup or the colour of a paper bag – and to be prepared to show it off. But don't display everyday things just for the sake of it. Select objects that have some emotional resonance for you; things that remind you of a time, a person or a place, for example. In this way you won't just be creating wallpaper but a meaningful personal display. Here, old postcards and photographs were stacked up in a silver toast rack to create an alternative and sculptural memento.

Playing with context. We tend to fill our homes with domestic things but by incorporating the odd eccentric everyday item into a furnishing scheme, we can add a quirky and innovative dimension to an interior and up its visual impact.

Bring in unexpectedly mundane objects to take the place of conventional furniture. For example, use rough-and-ready vegetable pallets as storage, old cleaning fluid bottles as vases (see the quick fix on page 133), bulldog clips as picture hooks. The key is to look twice at prosaic items to see if they can be used imaginatively in the home.

Moving the furniture around. We generally think of furniture as being room-specific. We put the wardrobe in the bedroom, for example, and the vegetable rack in the kitchen. But you can turn this convention on its head by using unexpected furniture in unexpected places. Use an ornate armoire for a larder and your kitchen will immediately seem more of a living room than a utility space; use a filing cabinet for storing clothes and you will add a funky industrial edge to any bedroom.

This displacement technique can work well on a small scale, too. Use a funky plastic fruit bowl for displaying your jewellery, or a shower curtain as a tablecloth. Good design should grab the eye wherever it is used and by giving it an unexpected role, you can only increase its impact.

New ways for old things. Recycling furniture and furnishings isn't just about being eco-friendly; if done well, it can bring cutting-edge looks to your living space, too. Think laterally and come up with innovative ways of re-using flea market finds or things you were about to throw away. Turn old jumpers or even tea-towels into offbeat cushions (see the Quick Fix on page 150); a naff 70s' mug-tree into a quirky lampbase. With a little imagination, you can make your junk funky, help protect the planet and save yourself money to boot.

Using the Extraordinary

A quirky piece of furniture or an unconventional material can make an interior, so when you come to furnish your home, think about incorporating the odd eccentric element. This is easier said than done, of course. Furnishing stores offer standard furniture, design shops sell conventional designer pieces; so where do you look for more unusual things for the home? The trick is to use the stylist's shopping list and to look off the beaten track.

Unconventional suppliers. Think lateral and consider kitting out your interior with bits and pieces sourced from commercial suppliers: for example, the places that equip offices, factories, churches. Their products are not intended for the domestic market, of course, and many commercial suppliers will be unused to dealing with public requests, so keep this in mind when you approach them (though they should offer a delivery service). Some may demand you buy materials in bulk (why not team up with your friends?); most are unlikely to offer conventional customer services. The advantage, however, is that commercial products are generally cheaper than their domestic counterparts and, by buying from an inconventional source you should be able to get an interesting and offbeat piece for your home at a good price.

The market for second-hand commercial kit is increasing rapidly, so it is worth keeping an eye out in fleamarkets, car boot sales, antique shops and local salvage yards for interesting old pieces. Alternatively, look in magazines for useful addresses, scour the Yellow Pages or the internet, or simply ask around for names of suppliers whose products you have seen locally. A little research can pay enormous dividends.

Furniture

Much modern furniture has a lateral spin, so tap into the latest design talent and choose one or two iconic and quirky pieces to give your interior an eccentric edge. Look for designs which play witty games with shape, form or material or use conventional pieces out of context. These chairs are by Dutch designer Ineke Hans.

Where to look

- Industrial catalogues: good for factory basics – cable reels, coffee tables.
- Catering suppliers: good for industrial-scaled kitchen kit – giant metal cookers, big fridges, overscaled pots and pans. Before you buy, make sure that any appliance you want to purchase will fit in your home (sometimes commercial and domestic gas pipes, for example, are different sizes) and that your saucepans won't be too small for the rings.
- Theatrical suppliers: particularly good for cheap and colourful velvet for curtains.
- Utility fabric shops: for heavy-duty materials such as deck-chair fabric, hessian and canvas, which will add texture to any home.
- Ships' chandlers: for colourful rope, thick cable (good for a funky curtain rail), portholes and much more.
- Shop fitters: for glass-fronted display furniture, clothes rails and shelves. Try to find one that specializes in second-hand shop fittings, which will generally be heavier, more interesting and better made than modern ones.

- Office suppliers: the best are those that deal in old stuff – wooden chests and filing cabinets, old architects' or dentists' chairs. The market for this kind of furniture has exploded in the last few years, so finding a bargain has become increasingly difficult. Try to keep off the beaten track and find local offices that are having a refit.
- Ecclesiastical suppliers: good for brilliantly coloured damasks (purple, emerald green, etc). Also look in shops that specialize in churchy regalia for giant church candles, overscaled candlesticks and old pews – great for a Gothic look or as a quirky one off.
- Laboratory suppliers: good for graphic and functional glassware to use for oils and vinegars, perhaps, or even for flowers.
- Builders' merchants: excellent for all manner of materials for DIY. For a funky look, use them raw: stack breeze blocks up to make a coffee table or room divider, for example.

Using Unexpected Materials

As well as furniture and furnishing fabrics, also think of sourcing the more basic materials for your home from commercial suppliers. Instead of buying conventional domestic carpets or linoleum for the floors, for example, consider the aluminium tread used on factory steps in the kitchen; the coarse carpeting used in car manufacture on a landing or in a hall. What were once strictly materials for the work place are now being welcomed in the domestic environment and new technology is constantly creating new fabrics for the home. So look around you for ideas and be adventurous – anything goes.

Glass and steel. Once the sole preserve of industrial or modernist buildings, these can give a functional, cool and modern flavour to any home. Don't just use them in utility spaces. Consider creating a see-through staircase up to a loft (check with experts first to make sure it is structurally possible) or include sleek metal furniture in a living room. Even a steel floor is a possibility, but expect to pay for the privilege.

Plastic and Perspex. These 20th-century materials will give an instant modern edge to any home and, of

The Industrial Look

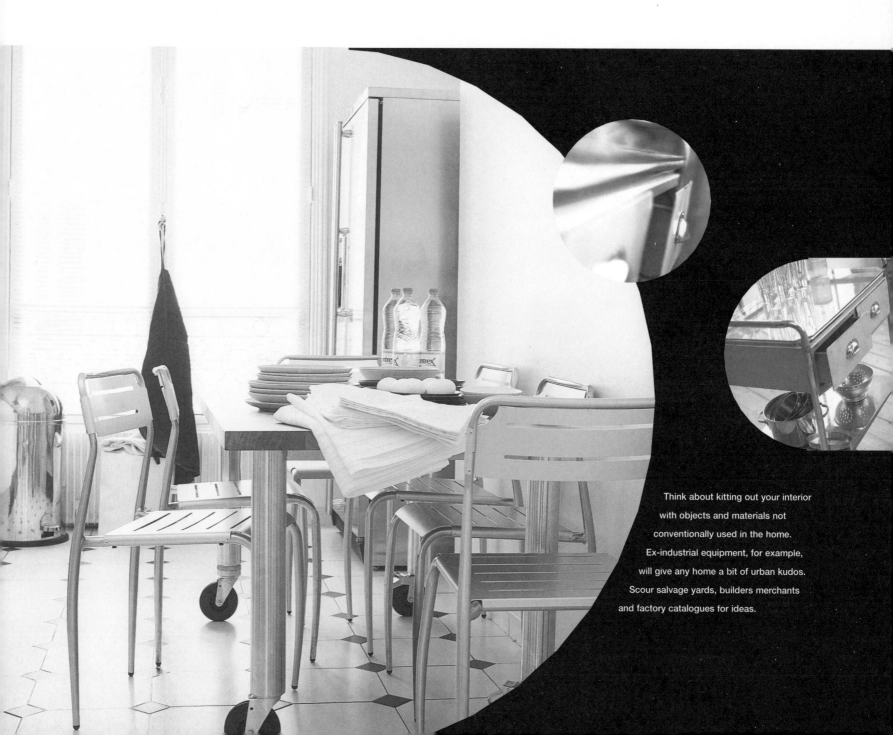

Think about kitting out your interior
with objects and materials not
conventionally used in the home.
Ex-industrial equipment, for example,
will give any home a bit of urban kudos.
Scour salvage yards, builders merchants
and factory catalogues for ideas.

Unconventional materials can make an interior, so think lateral and bring unexpected things inside. Recycled plastic sheeting (above) makes a brilliant and eco-friendly kitchen worktop. Old maps (right) make a witty alternative wallcovering.

Unexpected Materials

"Alternative wallpaper will add wit and visual texture to any room."

course, can add a good dose of colour, too. Think of using them in the structure of your interior partition between rooms, for example), or in the fittings. For a funky eco look, use sheets of recycled plastic for a kitchen worktop or a bathroom floor; for a new take on clothes storage, create an open wardrobe with clear Perspex rails. And don't forget the furniture: a curvy Perspex coffee table or a sinuous one-piece plastic chair will make any room look instantly modern.

Concrete and rubber. Traditionally used in hardcore industrial interiors, these two materials are fast becoming the latest must-have materials in the home. Use concrete for a cool kitchen worktop or even for the floor, but don't expect it to be cheap and make sure before you start that your floor or

kitchen units can bear the weight of it. Rubber is great for floors: it can cover up anything, is very soft on the feet and now comes in a range of brilliant colours and textures.

Simply eccentric. If you really want to get your neighbours talking, think about incorporating some very offbeat materials in the home. Use Astroturf or door-matting for a highly tactile floor; fibreglass for a shower; Neoprene (wet-suit fabric) for a sofa. Be as imaginative as you dare – just make sure whichever material you choose is viable in the space for which it is destined.

Outside In

One of the simplest and most subtle ways to give a quirky edge to your home is to bring outdoor things

inside. It's a lateral trick that is currently very fashionable and also one which is practical, easy and inexpensive to achieve. Think of incorporating garden fixtures and fittings into your interior or simply using natural found objects in the decoration. Consider making use of materials that are conventionally found externally – pebble-dash, for example, or render. And don't forget the plants – grasses, herbs and even vegetables grown inside will give any interior a flavour of the wild.

Top ten ideas

• Use pebble-dash inside your home to give unexpected texture, but don't overdo it: cover just one wall of a room as a contrast to the smoothness of the other three. Alternatively, for a more Mediterranean effect, stick pebbles into wet plaster

either on a wall or a floor.

• Lay decking inside the house – in a room that opens onto the garden, perhaps, to alleviate the problem of muddy feet.

• Bring external light fittings (generally bigger and less decorative than internal ones) inside for a modern, streamlined look.

• Use natural bamboo fencing as a screen or a room divider.

• Give your walls a rough seaside finish by covering them with plaster mixed with sand

• Simply display outdoor fittings inside: a traditional telephone box (if you are lucky enough to find one); a street sign (look in salvage yards); even a garden gnome (Philippe Starck has done just this in London Hotel, St Martin's Lane).

• Use trellis as a noticeboard or a room divider.

• Turn pieces of driftwood into naturally sculptural shelves.

• Use pebbles for paperweights.

• Transform a room into a grotto by lining the walls with shells or use quirky giant shells in the details (as a curtain finial, perhaps).

Where To Be Lateral

Every element of your home can benefit from a lateral approach, so keep it with you whatever room you are decorating. Don't feel you have to come up with hundreds of innovative ideas: just a couple will give your interior a fresh and exciting edge.

Walls and Floors

Conventionally, we make more of a statement with the contents of a room than with its background. The walls and the floor of an interior are often kept fairly plain to show off the rest, but these expansive surfaces can take expansive ideas and, if you really want a lateral look, they are the perfect place to experiment with the unexpected.

First consider unusual materials. Cover your walls up with maps, sheet music, fabric, brown paper, cork – whatever is appropriate to the room you are decorating. These alternatives to wallpaper will add wit and visual texture to any room. Cover the floor with leather, rubber, glass, metal, Astroturf – choose something that is as unexpected texturally as visually for maximum impact. Alternatively, put quirky pictures on the floor using laminated cork tiles (several suppliers can custom-make these with your own specified image).

Think, too, about alternative ways to apply your materials. Create graphic patterns on the wall with paint or paper and on the floor with whatever flooring you have chosen. Create a wave effect with different coloured carpet, perhaps, or lay rubber flooring like a patchwork or even a jigsaw puzzle. It is worth bearing in mind, of course, that a complicated wall or floor scheme will make for a visually complicated room, so keep any busier

Outside In

"Bringing outdoor elements inside is easy to do and very effective."

patterns for parts of your home with few other visual stimuli (the hall or landing, for example).

Lateral Ideas for all around the House

In the kitchen

- Replace dull drawer handles and cupboard pulls with something a little less conventional: forks, twigs, rope – anything goes.
- Revamp old kitchen units by changing the doors and consider new materials – wire mesh, coloured or frosted glass, Perspex. Alternatively, cover them up with metallic spray, blackboard paint (great for shopping lists) or even fake gold.
- Make use of industrial materials for worktops and floors: recycled plastic, industrial metal sheeting, concrete or even resin – an expensive option.

- Spray an old fridge or cooker in a brilliant colour with car paint (if you do it in situ, cover up the rest of the room very carefully to avoid getting colour everywhere).
- Put wheels on your appliances and units. This will look very funky and makes for easy cleaning.

In the living room

- Instead of stripping down ugly wallpaper, cover it up with plain white paper cut with circular holes for a graphic 'peephole' look.
- Replace conventional curtains with more unexpected window coverings: Indian saris for colour, bamboo matting for texture, a length of fleece or felt for warmth.
- Alternatively, screen your windows more permanently by frosting the glass (see the quick fix on page 49) or covering panes with coloured vinyl film (this can be peeled off when you feel like a change).
- Use alternative curtain tiebacks: a thread of beads, a length of ribbon or rope, an old scarf or even a dog collar.
- Use ribbon curtains for doors or at windows (see the quick fix on page 114).
- Sew together old jeans to make a fashionable sofa (or get it re-upholstered in denim for a tighter result).

In the bedroom

- For an industrial look, make a scaffolding frame for your divan or place it on old vegetable pallets. To revamp an old bed, customize it with a canvas or MDF bedhead.
- Make personalized bedlinen by having your

Walls and Floors

Make a statement underfoot with a figurative floor covering. Buy ready-made or get your own design made up for a bespoke and individual result.

favourite images printed on to sheets or pillowcases (simply photocopy an image you like onto transfer paper and go to a copy shop).

- Get your sheets or pillowcases monogrammed with a name or a special message.
- Think of alternative covers for your bed: a length of lace, fake fur or a large sheepskin rug.
- Use old utility furniture for clothes storage.

In the bathroom

- Use the side of the bath as display space for photographs or your favourite images (get them laminated to make them waterproof and slide between sheets of glass or Perspex cut to fit the size of the original bath panel).
- In a small bathroom, consider putting shelves against the window to give you privacy and extra storage space.
- Be creative with your loo rolls. Display eight or twelve rolls on a wall, (hung from metal hooks or Perspex rods) for a witty everyday installation.

Lateral Lighting

A fundamental part of any living space, lighting has enormous decorative potential which is rarely exploited to the full in the home. When it comes to creating a scheme, don't stick to glaring overhead lamps and A-line shades; be imaginative. Think about what kind of lighting you want in each room of the house and look around for new and interesting ways to achieve it.

These days it is fairly easy to unearth innovative and unconventional lights and lamps at both ends of the price scale, from eccentric pieces by lighting guru Ingo Maurer (his 'Porca Miseria' chandelier is made up of broken crockery, for example) to funky and informal contemporary pieces like Tom Dixon's plastic 'Jack' lights (see page 82) or inflatable plastic lights by British design company Inflate.

Lateral Light

British design company Inflate make everything from blow-up fruit bowls to these Space Age lights — perfect for adding a lateral edge to any interior.

Brilliant for transforming a dull corner, these simple geometric paper lights (above and right) are more like sculptures than anything purely functional.

Light Displays

"Treat light creatively to maximise its decorative potential."

Consider, too, how to treat light itself creatively. Keep your eyes open in hotels, shops or art galleries for ingenious lighting displays and think how you could apply them in your own home. Use coloured light to 'paint' elements of your interior – an alcove or a panel of wall, perhaps – or create patterns of light and shade with clever directional lighting. Also think about hanging your lights in unconventional ways to give a room an individual edge

Finally, if you can afford it, buy the odd light sculpture: the millennial equivalent of the old master.

Tips for alternative lighting

• Instead of one central pendant light, hang a series. This will take the focus away from one spot on the ceiling and give you an intimate ambient effect.

• Show off your bare bulbs. Make them big and silver-bottomed, if you like, or hang them in a bunch to make a quirky installation.

• Line up three or more strips of neon (coloured or white) for a brilliant light feature. Alternatively, prop a few free-standing neon stick lights against the wall to transform a dull corner.

• Re-think those fairy lights: drape them along a mantelpiece, display them vertically on a wall or around a door (using masking tape or a small hook to attach them at the top) or even stretch them down the middle of a dining table for a dramatic centrepiece (but watch out for the cable).

• Think up unusual ways to use a standard shade. Stack three or four on top of each other to make a sculptural floor lamp, for example, or if you can, use them upside down.

• Consider revamping old shades or customizing new ones to give them that personal touch. Cover them up with wrapping paper (see the Quick Fix on page 148), or fabric; wrap them with raffia, ribbon or even string; stencil or paint them with graphic patterns.

• Make your own shades out of sculpted wire mesh (see the Quick Fix on page 128)

• Display light boxes on the wall (see page 105) or even on the side of the bath to make a quirky glowing panel.

• Top a lampbase with something a little more unusual than a shade – a hat, perhaps, or a colander (make sure you spray any fabric with some sort of fire retardant first).

• Think up innovative ways to display your candles – behind Perspex panels, perhaps, or in a tight line all along a shelf or mantelpiece (see page 104).

Quick Fixes

Every element of your home can benefit from a lateral approach but don't try too hard to be alternative. Here are eight quick fixes which will give your interior a lateral spin without making it look self-conscious or over-styled.

Great Slates

"For an alternative tabletop, be creative with slate."

YOU WILL NEED

Slate tiles (from tile shops or roofing suppliers)
Sticky-backed felt sheeting
Chalk

Simply attach sticky-backed felt or small sticky pads to the back of the slate tile (this is to protect the surface of the table) and chalk on the name of your guest or a special message.

→ Stylist tip. If you have difficulty finding slate tiles, contact local quarries and get slate slabs cut to size. Also, think of other unusual materials for mats: bamboo matting; thick felt or coloured cork or laminated photographs, for example.

"Give your floor or table lamp
a facelift with a streamlined
metal shade."

Wraparound Shade

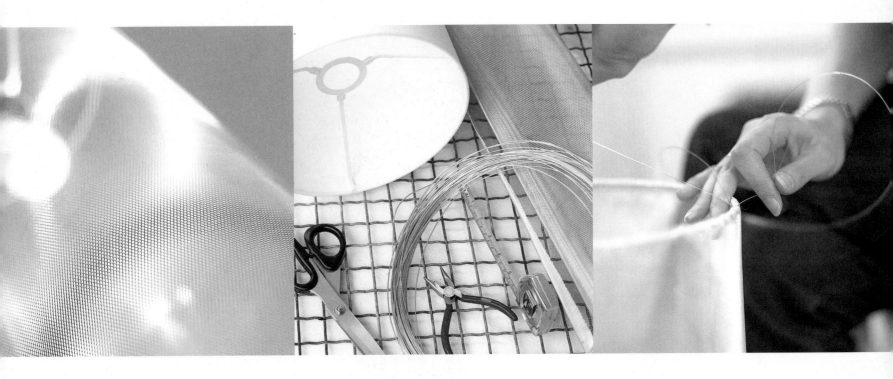

YOU WILL NEED

1 x old straight-sided lampshade

Fine flexible stainless steel or copper wire mesh
(available from most hardware stores)

Roll of fine wire

1   Take the fabric off the existing shade and discard.

2   Measure the shade and cut a length of wire mesh a little larger than you need (allow around 3– 4cm/2in – extra at the top, bottom and sides).

3   Wrap the mesh around the frame and secure the top and the bottom by folding the mesh over the frame of the shade and securing in place with fine wire (you can do this by threading the wire in and out of the small holes of the mesh).

4   For the side 'seam', overlap the wire mesh and secure in the same way, making sure to tuck in any sharp wire ends and cut off any excess mesh.

→   **Stylist tip.** You should be able to find wire mesh in different grades, so choose the one you like best. You can pull it taut for a smooth effect (as here) or crumple it like paper to make a more sculptural shade in any shape you like.

Idea from Melinda Ashton Turner.

Dishy Centrepiece

"Think lateral and raid your cupboards to make an instant and eye-catching tablecentre."

YOU WILL NEED

White taper candles
Dishwasher salt
Glass vase

Simply fill a clear glass vase with dishwasher salt and place white taper candles (available from most good candle shops or department stores) inside.

Idea from Rebecca Duke.

Wooden Block Furniture

" Wooden blocks make instant modular furniture that will look good anywhere."

YOU WILL NEED

Wooden blocks (try local timber yards for recycled
    pieces or call a local tree surgeon who may
    be able to supply old tree trunks)
Sandpaper

Simply get the wood cut to the size you require
and sand it smooth. Then use all around the house
as a seat, or a side-table.

Cork Cube

"An instant update for an old table."

YOU WILL NEED

Old piece of furniture

**Self-adhesive cork tiles (available from most
    good DIY stores)**

This must be the easiest way to revamp a boring
piece of furniture. Simply clean the surfaces, peel
the backing paper from the cork tiles and stick on
where required.

➔   **Stylist tip.** We used an old plastic
storage cube, but cork tiles would work just as
well on a coffee-table top or a bedside table.

Idea from Emma Thomas.

Brilliant Bottles

"Recycling has never looked so good."

YOU WILL NEED

Old plastic cleaning fluid bottles, washed thoroughly and with labels soaked off.

Choose a selection of bottles in different colours and shapes, fill with flowers (or not) and group for a brilliantly kitsch shelf or table display.

Idea from Sarah Hollywood.

Ribbon Curtain

YOU WILL NEED

1 x ribbon curtain (available from most
  hardware stores)
Tape measure

"A funky and fun way to dress up a doorway."

1 Dividing rooms with a ribbon curtain rather than a solid door is a brilliant way to save space in a small house. Most come on an extendable pole and are easy to fit. Measure the doorway first to make sure the curtain will fit snugly in the space.

➡ **Stylist tip.** For a more decorative effect, use a bead curtain (make your own if you can't find one). Or use ribbon curtains at the window to give you privacy without losing light.

Idea from Melinda Ashton Turner.

DIY Desk Tidy

YOU WILL NEED

Bricks (salvaged from building work or bought
   from a DIY store)
Spray paint
Newspaper

1 Lay bricks on newspaper to protect the surrounding area and spray with paint (use lots of thin layers and allow to dry in between to avoid drip marks) until you have a thick glassy finish with no brick showing through. Leave to dry overnight and then use for all those odd bits and pieces on the desktop.

→   **Stylist tip.** Choose a colour that co-ordinates or clashes with your office and stack the bricks up for a different effect.

Today our homes have become as much a fashion statement as our wardrobes. Furniture and furnishings – things we once bought for life – have become as ephemeral in appeal as their sartorial cousins. The media, ever eager for something new, presents us with looks for the home that change season by season (if not month by month) and even retailers – previously a conservative bunch – have started to follow suit. Now it seems that not only do we need to furnish our homes comfortably and stylishly, but keep them up to date, too.

This isn't as futile as it sounds. It would be foolish (and expensive, of course) to jump on the treadmill of taste and follow all the vagaries of interior trends, but fashion does have an important role to play in the home. Today's interior shouldn't be stagnant and inflexible, somewhere that will look the same in ten years' time as it does now; rather, it should be alive and evolving; somewhere that can embrace the new and move with the times. Injecting a bit of fashion into a living space can be the best way of giving it verve and vitality.

First, keep yourself informed of what's in and what's out by reading lifestyle magazines and looking at the latest furnishing collections. Keep an eye on high-street fashion, too: the interior world makes a habit of stealing ideas straight from the catwalk. Think about what you like and how you can introduce elements of the latest looks into your home. Be discerning and don't be a slave to fashion. Remember, many of today's must-haves will turn out to be tomorrow's has-beens.

Don't feel you have to makeover your entire interior: the trick is to update your space in the details – to accessorize a room with a designer vase, perhaps, or a funky fabric – much as you would spruce up last year's outfit with the latest beaded bag or throw. Even one iconic fashion item can make all the difference. And don't feel you always have to buy new. Work with what you've got and think of cheap and easy ways of

Keep Up To Date

giving your furniture a fashionable edge – by reupholstering a sofa in a new material, for example, or by sewing the latest trimming onto the edge of a cushion. With a little imagination, you can keep your home at the cutting edge with minimum effort and cost.

Keep it Moving

A furnished interior is not a finished interior, so don't fall into the trap of forgetting about your surroundings once you have done the decorating. Keep a room alive by moving around the contents (month-by-month perhaps), by taking away the out of date and adding the new. This needn't be a difficult nor an expensive task. Changing a

mantelpiece display or throwing new cushions on a sofa can instantly update a room.

Build yourself a core collection of classic furniture (it doesn't need to be expensive) which can be dressed up with the latest fashions season by season (much like the little black dress); and keep the background of a room (walls, floors and ceilings) fairly plain so you can instantly update the space with a coat of the latest colour or a panel of modish wallpaper.

To make it easier, allot just one part of a room for the fashion treatment (the mantelpiece, perhaps, or just one wall). This way, you will minimize the effort but give yourself the flexibility to introduce a few new pieces whenever you feel like it.

Show Off Your Labels

Fashion hit the home most dramatically in the late 90s when many of the big names in the fashion world started launching home collections. First there was Ralph Lauren, then Calvin Klein, Donna Karan, Nicole Farhi and many others. Suddenly the interiors world was swamped with fashionable furnishings: as well as dressing in designer clothes, we could eat from designer plates and sit on designer stools; we could have, in essence, a designer lifestyle.

What these collections offer is a way to inject fashion instantly into our homes; a way to dress up an interior with cutting-edge details. So rather than buying in a complete designer look (and bankrupting yourself in the process), treat yourself to just one or

Fashion Details

Six easy ways to update your space

• Frame a panel of fabric in the latest colour on a wall and simply switch it when the fashion changes.

• Disguise an old armchair with a throw made out of fashionable fabric.

• Use a length of the latest fabric as a table runner (great for dinner parties) and simply change when you want a new look.

• Buy cheap and trendy rugs to transform a room instantly.

• See which blooms have hit the big time and fill your home with fashionable flowers.

• Don't chuck out your sofa; just buy or make new cushions.

"Dress up your furniture in the latest fabrics."

two pieces. A single, beautifully designed ceramic vase from Nicole Farhi, for example, will lift a living room; a Calvin Klein plate, instantly update a tabletop. What's more, one designer piece may inspire you to create a new look for your whole interior.

Don't chuck out the bags. If you can't afford the fashion products, just display the packaging. Most designer outlets have designer bags (usually in great colours), so buy the most inexpensive thing you can from Gucci, Christian Lacroix, Hermès or wherever and simply show off the outer wrapping it came in.

Stealing Catwalk Ideas
Keep up-to-date with what's happening on the catwalk and think of ways to introduce the latest fashion ideas into your home.

Consider using dress material rather than upholstery fabric for your furniture or curtains. It may not last quite as long, but you'll probably pay less and get cutting-edge looks into the bargain (make sure to spray it with a fire retardant first if it isn't flameproof). Alternatively, just run up a couple of cushions in the latest prints and re-cover when the fashion changes.

Visit your local haberdashery and stock up on trendy trimmings – feathers, ribbons, buttons, beads – which will add an instant fashion element to every part of your home. Edge sofas and armchairs with funky fringing; sew a velvet ribbon onto a silk sheet; beads or buttons onto a curtain. Don't accessorize everything: remember that subtlety works best. Even a row of feathers simply lined up on a tabletop will give a room a touch of catwalk kudos.

Sartorial Style
As today's stylish interior is an integrated place where fashion and furnishing merge, it makes sense to bring your clothes out of the closet. We've all been wooed by images in those styled magazine interiors of covetably understated rooms with a beautiful dress hung on the back of a door or a pair of shapely shoes nonchalantly thrown across a sheepskin rug. This isn't real life, of course; it is simply something the stylist does to make an interior look fashionable and lived in; but as it looks so good, why not do it in our own homes?

Instead of hiding your designer dresses in the cupboard, put them on display; hang a collection on Perspex rails or single out one striking piece and display it in isolation against a cupboard (choose a different item each week so it doesn't gather dust).

**Bring your clothes out of the closet.
A designer dress hung on a door, for
example, will give your bedroom instant
catwalk kudos.**

There is something to be said for keeping some clothes behind closed doors (that velour tracksuit for one), but this treatment isn't just reserved for haute couture. Even the simplest things, well displayed, can look graphic and offbeat. A row of raw linen shirts against a chalky wall, for example; a vivid Chinese dress on a glossy door; a quirky antique shoe on a step – these can make as much of an impact as any more recherché designer clothing.

Think, too, about displaying fashion accessories – gloves, hats and handbags, for example. These cost considerably less and can easily be changed when you want to update your interior.

Quick fashion tips

• Reupholster the seats of your dining chairs in the latest fashion fabrics (if they lift out, you can simply staple-gun the new fabric to the bottom of the seat).

• Make up your own cushion covers in modish materials such as leather, denim or Chinese silk. Buy remnants in fabric shops to save money.

• Stitching is back in vogue, so get out your needle and thread and sew graphic stars onto a silk sheet or blanket-stitch the edge of a cushion or throw.

• Trimmings are in, so add them to everything from cushions to lampshades.

• Make up a throw in a funky fabric.

• Give your curtains the latest hemline (whether it is fringed, geometric or curved).

• Use catwalk combinations of colour and fabric: denim and leather for a cowboy look, or velvet and lace for a vintage feminine feel.

Sartorial Style

Quick Fixes

Here are six fashionable fixes which will give your interior cutting-edge looks without a designer price tag.

Get a Look: Chinese

YOU WILL NEED

Low bench table in wood
Floor cushions to sit on
Oriental tableware in dark colours
Chopsticks
Chinese lanterns
An Oriental image

Easy and inexpensive to achieve, a Chinese look is the height of fashion. Raid Oriental stores for ideas and supplies, but don't go over the top. Keep the background plain and the furniture simple, low-level and natural. Colour can come in the details – a cushion in a vivid Chinese fabric, for example, or a selection of garish paper lanterns, hung at different heights.

→ **Stylist tip.** You can use any transparent or translucent material as long as it is stiff enough. Why stop at images – display leaves, stamps, material, or anything 2-D that takes your fancy.

"Revamp an old lamp
with a funky new shade."

Designer Light

YOU WILL NEED

Newspaper

Cheap lamp from a DIY store (or an old one)

Spray paint in colour of choice

Wrapping or art paper

Craft knife or scissors

Tape measure

Spray glue

1 Protect the worksurface with a layer of newspaper. Take the lampshade off the base and spray the base with paint (we used Plasti-kote which can be used on virtually any surface). Build up colour with a series of thin layers of paint to avoid drip marks. Leave to dry.

2 Meanwhile, measure the shade and cut your chosen covering paper to fit, allowing 2–3 cm (¾–1 in) overlap at the sides and the top.

3 Working in a well-ventilated area, spray the paper with glue and carefully wrap around the shade, ironing out bubbles with your hand as you do so (it is easier to do this on a flat surface).

4 Trim the excess paper from the shade with scissors or a craft knife and position the new shade on the base.

→ **Stylist tip.** You can revamp any old lamps like this and use a variety of coverings. As well as different kinds of wrapping and coloured paper, you could try newspaper, maps or even fabric.

Idea from Emma Thomas.

Cutting-edge Cushions

1 Cut off the sleeves and neckline of the jumper, turn it inside out and, using matching wool, sew up the armholes and top to make a square.

2 Turn the jumper right side out again and insert a suitably-sized cushion pad. Tuck the ends in, pin and carefully stitch up the final seam using matching wool.

1 Fold tea towel in half and sew up the two side edges to fit pad. (To make a bigger cover use two tea towels and stitch around three sides.)

2 Turn tea towel right side out again, insert pad and carefully stitch up the final seam.

1 Jazz up a plain cushion with a length of suede fringing (or any other trimming you like). Simply lay out in a pattern on the front of your cushion and neatly sew top of trimming to cushion cover (take the pad out first and be careful not to stitch two sides of the cover together).

➡ **Stylist tip.** Think of turning other fashion fabrics into textural cushions. Use the denim from a pair of old jeans, for example, or create a patchwork with remnants of the latest prints.

YOU WILL NEED

Cushion pads*

Old woollen jumpers

Tea towels

Trimmings – fringing, ribbon or braid.

Wool (to match the colour of the jumper)

Needle and cotton

*Before you buy a cushion pad, measure the

tea towel and the body of the chosen jumper

to work out what size you will need.

"Turn jumble-sale jumpers and tea-towels into cutting-edge cushions or update old ones with new trimmings."

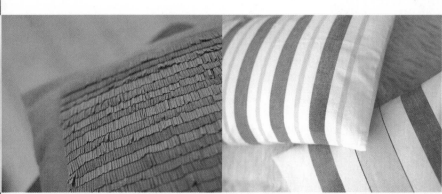

YOU WILL NEED

A length of MDF cut to fit the width of your bed and
    as high as you require

Stretch wadding (around 1.5cm/4in thick) or thin foam

Staple gun (these can be hired)

Fabric wide enough to cover bedhead without a join

Battens (optional)

Screws or very strong wood glue (optional)

Bespoke Bedhead

1 Get a length of MDF cut to the required size (a builder's merchant or DIY store should be able to do this for you).

2 Stretch wadding over the front of the board and staple-gun to the back. Alternatively, cut thin foam to the size of the board and glue in place.

3 Staple one end of your chosen fabric to the back of the board and then stretch it over the padding carefully and staple in place at the other end. Make it as taut as possible to avoid wrinkles (it is easiest to do this with two people).

4 Once the sides are attached, staple the fabric to the back of the board at the top and the bottom (doing hospital corners to make it neat).

5 Simply stand the bedhead behind the bed or, for a more permanent solution, attach it to the wall or the bed base. You can do this by fixing wooden battens to the bedhead on either side and then attaching these to the base of the bed with screws or strong glue.

➡ **Stylist tip.** Be imaginative in your choice of fabric. Here we used pink satin, but you could choose a heavyweight material such as hessian or colourful felt (these would be less likely to fray, too).

"Transform an old bed with a brilliant new headboard."

Easy Art

YOU WILL NEED

A panel of MDF or hardboard
Wallpaper or fabric
Paper or wood glue

1 Trawl charity shops and car boot sales to find old lengths of funky fabric or rolls of retro wallpaper, or buy new.

2 Get a piece of MDF cut to the width of the wallpaper or fabric and to whatever length you require. Then glue the covering onto the board with strong paper/wood glue.

3 Spray the finished artwork with varnish to protect the surface and, when dry, hang on the wall as a graphic work of art.

→ **Stylist tip.** Alternatively, simply stretch your fabric or paper over a wooden frame and staple-gun in place.

Idea from Lucy Dunn, deputy editor of *Living Etc*.

"An easy and cheap way to make your own art."

YOU WILL NEED

2 low bolsters to sit on

Paper lantern

Low bench table

Japanese-style crockery in black

Flower heads to float in water

An incense burner and incense sticks

Keep the look pure and simple with an emphasis on natural textures and simple Oriental shapes. Choose pared down tableware in black, red or deep green and supplement with rush or paper mats, chopsticks and incense (though not when you are eating). This low-level look works brilliantly in the bedroom, too. Substitute a conventional bed for a futon (or just place your divan on the floor) and keep furnishings minimal, natural and unfussy.

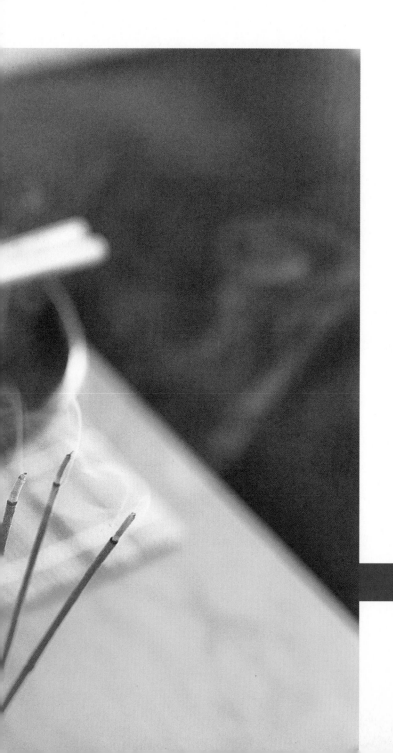

A

Aalto, Alvar   34
alcove   80, 81
Arad, Ron   66
areas of display   80–89
ascending scale   70
asymmetry   73–74

B

background, one-colour   39
bags, designer   143
balance   72, 73–7
bathrooms   22, 86, 86–7, 122
bedrooms   22–3, 120–22
Bocca sofa   36
Bookworm shelving   25, 66
Brancusi, Constantin   66

C

Calder, Alexander   91
catwalk ideas   143
ceiling   91
Chinese Look   146–7
Christmas decoration   46–7
chronology of colour   40
clothes, displaying   59, 144–5
clutter-free living   18–19, 20–23
colour   38–45, 92
Columbo, Joe   36
concrete   117
context   112
cushions   143

D

Dada artists   110
descending scale   70
designer labels   140–3
display   54–105
Dixon, Tom   122
Duchamp, Marcel   110

E

Eames, Charles and Ray   34
Emin, Tracey   110
everyday sculpture   108–9, 108–11

F

Farhi, Nicole   140
Feng Shui   66
fifties look   32–3, 35–6
fireplace   55, 61, 62–3, 84–5
floors   88–91, 118–20
flowers   92–7, 93, 95, 97
form and shape   58–73
furniture   84–6, 112, 113
    Wooden Block   131

G

geometrical shapes   58–63
geometry   58–64
glass   117
Gormley, Anthony 70
Guild, Tricia   83

H

Hamilton, Richard   110
Hepworth, Barbara   66
Holding Company, The   20

Home Collections   140
Hoppen, Kelly   27

I

industrial look   112–15, 115
Ineke, Hans   113
Inflate   122–3

J

Jacobsen, Arne   34, 66
'Jack' light   82, 122
Jackson, Janie   16, 17,
Japanese look   154–5
junk, using   112

K

Karan, Donna   140
kitchen   20, 120
Klein, Calvin   140

L

Lauren, Ralph   140
lava lamp   66
light   17
lighting   122–5, 123, 124, 128–9
living room   20, 120
London Hotel   118
look
    Chinese   146–7
    fifties   32–3, 35–6
    industrial   112–15, 115
    Japanese   154–5
    mid-century modern   34–5
    monotone   40–42
    Oriental   26–7
    period   32–8

seventies   37, 38

sixties   36–8

two tone   42–3

M

Macdonald, Ruth   74

mantelpiece   80–83, 82–3

Maurer, Ingo   122

mid-century modern look   34–5

minimalism   16, 17

mobiles   92

modernist   30–31

monotone look   40–42

Moore, Henry   66

Mourgue, Olivier   36

mushroom chair   34–5

O

office, clutter-free   20–22

organic shapes   64–5, 64–8, 67

Oriental look   26–7

outdoor things   66, 117–8, 117–8

oversize   70–73, 71

P

Panton, Verner   35

paring down   19–24

Paulin, Pierre   35–6

period look   32–8

Perspex   114, 117, 120, 122

pictures, creating   78–9

placemats   126–7

Porca Miseria chandelier   122

Polo chairs   62

Pop Art   109, 110

Q

Quick Fixes

Bespoke Bedhead   152

Brilliant Bottles   133

Cork Cube   132

Cutting-edge Cushions   150–51

Designer Light   148–49

Dishy Centrepiece   130

DIY Desk Tidy   134–5

Easy Art   153

Easy Picture Frames   98–9

Festive Foliage   47

Funky Mousemats   103

Get a Look: Chinese   146

Get a Look: Japanese   154–5

Graphic Glasses   48–9

Great Slates   126–7

Instant Art   100–101

Named Napkin Rings   51

Personalised Notebooks   102

Pocket Calendar   50

Ribbon Curtain   134

Spotlights   104–5

Wooden Block Furniture   131

Wraparound Shade   128–9

R

recycling   112, 133

repetition   74

rubber   117

S

Saarinen, Eero   34

scale   68–73, 69

Schwitters, Kurt   110

sculpture, everyday   108–11, 108–9

seventies look   37, 38

shape

and flowers   94

and form   58–73

simplicity   16–51

sixties look   36–8

size   68–70

Sottsass, Ettore   36

space-age style   66

Starck, Philippe   118

steel   117

storage   20–21, 24–6

Studio 65   36

symmetry   73

T

texture   45

themes   28–32

two tone look   42–3

U

undersize   70

unexpected materials   114–18, 116–17

up to date, keeping   138–40

W

walls   86–8, 88–90, 118–20

Walter, Dawna   20, 23

Wegner, Hans   34

Z

Zanotta   36

publisher's acknowledgements

All photography by Ray Main/Mainstream, except for the following:

70: Ocean; **95**: Clay Perry; **100–101**: images copied from the book of the film *The Red Balloon*, published by Doubleday, Random House. Images used courtesy of Films Montsouris, Paris; **113**: Dutch Individuals Foundation; **122–3**: Inflate; **137**: Designers Guild.

Ray Main would like to thank the following for their permission to reproduce images: **20–1**, **38–39**, **60–61**, **145**: Babylon Design; **2**, **30–1**: Patrick Gwynne; **2**, **60–61**: Gregory Phillips; **60**: *left* Mary Thum Architects; **79**: Mark Guard; **88**: *left* FAT Architects; **88**: *middle* Kelly Hoppen; **108–109**: Lawrence Llewelyn-Bowen.

The publisher has endeavoured to get permission to reproduce all the photographs in this publication. If we have unwittingly overlooked any, we sincerely apologise and will be pleased to rectify the situation in all forthcoming editions.

We would also like to thank the following for supplying props for photoshoots and/or locations for photoshoots: 2021; Aero; Alma Home; Ashwell Recyling; Marian Cotterall; Habitat; Janie Jackson; Judy Greenwood Antiques; Cath Kidston; Michael Loates-Taylor and Elaine Toogood at Loates Taylor Shannon; Ming Mang; Neal Street East; Regalian; Retro Home; Space; Ottilie Stevenson; Patrick Stockley Studios; Sam Chapman at Taylor Woodrow; The Cross; The Flower Van; Urban Outfitters; Vessel; Christina Wilson.

author's acknowledgements

With special thanks to Kyle Cathie, Kate Oldfield, and Helen Woodhall, Kevin Knight and Joanna Carton at Button Design; photographer Ray Main and his assistant Owen; stylists Victoria Barker and Emma Thomas; Gillian Haslam and Gill and Mick Hodson. Thanks, too, to the stylists who contributed Quick Fixes and to Terence Conran, Tricia Guild, Kelly Hoppen and Dawna Walter who kindly contributed quotes for the book.

Thanks to Patrick Brillet for his helpful article in *Elle Decoration* UK, No. 59, May 1997; Sue Parker at Habitat UK for the idea of turning a gourd into a lampbase and creating a band of postcards around the walls of a room; Gijs Bakker for the idea of covering up ugly wallpaper with plain white paper cut with holes which first appeared in *Elle Decoration* UK, No. 41 and Jane Withers for the idea of using a dog collar as a curtain tieback. Thanks also to *Elle Decoration* UK and *The Sunday Times* for permission to reproduce quotes from Carolyn Quartermaine, Andy Martin and Ruth Macdonald.